Raising Intelligent Muslim Children

Muddassir Khan

Published by Muddassir Khan, 2024.

Table of Contents

Raising Intelligent Muslim Children

Muddassir Khan

While every precaution has been taken in the preparation of this book, the publisher assumes no responsibility for errors or omissions, or for damages resulting from the use of the information contained herein.

Introduction

Praise be to Allah. We praise Him, seek His help, ask for His forgiveness, and seek refuge in Allah from the evils of ourselves and the misdeeds of our actions. Whomever Allah guides, no one can mislead; and whomever He leaves astray, no one can guide. I bear witness that there is no deity but Allah, alone with no partners, and I bear witness that Muhammad is His servant and messenger. May Allah's peace and blessings be upon him, his family, his companions, and those who follow them with righteousness until the Day of Judgment.

Parental love for children is a profound and intrinsic quality, rooted in deep-seated psychological feelings and a natural sense of compassion. This innate disposition compels parents to protect, show mercy, sympathize, and care for their children. Without such love and patience, humanity would face dire consequences, as parents would be unable to nurture, guide, and support their offspring.

The Noble Qur'an vividly illustrates these parental emotions. For example, Allah (the Most High) says in Surah Al-Kahf:

"Wealth and children are the adornment of the life of this world..." (18:46).

This verse emphasizes that children are among the greatest blessings and adornments of worldly life.

In another instance, Surah Al-Isra reveals Allah's gratitude for His blessings, including children:

"We helped you with wealth and children and made you more numerous in man-power." (17:6).

Moreover, in Surah Al-Furqan, Allah (the Most High) describes the prayers of the righteous for their children to be a source of comfort and joy:

"And those who say: 'Our Lord! Bestow on us from our wives and our offspring the comfort of our eyes, and make us leaders of the Muttaqun.'" (25:74).

The love and care of parents are also exemplified in the stories of the Prophets. For instance, Prophet Ibrahim (peace be upon him) displayed immense love and patience while raising his sons, particularly Isma'il (peace be upon him). Despite the immense test of being commanded to sacrifice his son, Prophet Ibrahim's (peace be upon him) profound trust in Allah and his enduring love for Isma'il (peace be upon him) highlight the deep bond between them. This story reflects the ultimate submission to Allah's will and the strength of parental devotion.

Similarly, the Prophet Muhammad (peace and blessings of Allah be upon him) demonstrated exceptional parental love and compassion. His relationship with his daughter Fatimah (Allah be pleased with her) is a testament to this. The Prophet (peace and blessings of Allah be upon him) showed great affection and concern for Fatimah (Allah be pleased with her) and supported her throughout her life. His Hadith, "The best of you are those who are best to their women" (Sunan Ibn Majah, 1856), underscores the importance of treating one's children and family with kindness and respect.

These examples from the Qur'an and the lives of the Prophets illustrate the deep and inherent bond between parents and their children. They serve as a guide to understanding the sanctity and importance of this relationship, emphasizing the need to cherish and nurture this divine gift.

Chapter 1

———

Religious education begins by introducing the child, as soon as they start to grasp the concept of faith, to the principles of Islam. This involves teaching the child the pillars of Islam and the foundation of the Shahadah, instilling a connection with the essence of their religion. The foundation of faith is grounded in belief in Allah, the Most High, His Angels, His Books, His Messengers, the Last Day, and Divine predestination. The pillars of Islam involve testifying that there is no deity worthy of worship except Allah and that Muhammad (peace and blessings of Allah be upon him) is His final Messenger, establishing prayer (salah), fasting during Ramadan, giving Zakah, and performing Hajj for those who are able. By Shari'ah, we mean everything that encompasses Islam—creed, worship, manners, and rulings.

Consider Fatimah, who began teaching her children the Shahadah as soon as they could speak. Each morning, they recited "La ilaha illallah" and "Muhammadur Rasulullah" together. This daily practice planted the seeds of faith in her children's hearts from a very young age, embedding the essence of iman in their upbringing.

Teaching Children Tawheed

Starting early is key when teaching children about Tawheed (the Oneness of Allah). Lessons should be age-appropriate, emphasizing Allah's ability to hear and see everything. As children mature, they must understand that their good deeds are rewarded by Allah and that living by Islamic principles is necessary.

The Prophet (peace and blessings of Allah be upon him) demonstrated this by teaching these concepts to young companions, such as 'Abdullah ibn 'Abbas: "O young man, I will teach you some words: Be mindful of Allah, and Allah will protect you. Be mindful of Allah, and you will find Him before you. If you ask, ask Allah; if you seek help, seek help from Allah..." (Tirmidhi).

For instance, Ibrahim, a father of two young boys, often reminded them that Allah watches over them at all times. During a family trip, when they watched a beautiful sunset together, Ibrahim asked his sons, "Who made the sun rise?" His guidance helped them reflect on the greatness of Allah, the Most High, and recognize Him as the Creator of all things.

Understanding Allah's Blessings

Children should also be taught to appreciate the countless blessings from Allah. Parents can ask questions like, "Who gave you your eyes to see and your ears to hear?" to nurture gratitude towards Allah.

For example, Amina, a mother of three, regularly reminded her children to say "Alhamdulillah" whenever they received any blessing. When her son fell ill, she taught him to thank Allah for his recovery after he got better. This practice instilled an appreciation for Allah's blessings, and soon after, the child began reminding his mother to say "Alhamdulillah" whenever either of them recovered from any illness.

Addressing Children's Questions About Allah

Children often ask profound questions, such as, "Does Allah eat or sleep?" This curiosity presents an opportunity to instill a deeper understanding of the uniqueness of Allah. When Sara's daughter asked whether Allah needed sleep like humans, Sara explained that Allah, as the Quran says, is unlike anything in creation and is the All-Hearing, All-Seeing (42:11). She emphasized that Allah does not need to eat or sleep, reinforcing the understanding of His unmatched power and distinct nature.

Instilling the Spirit of Submission

One of the most important aspects of Islamic education is teaching children submission to Allah. This can be achieved by showing them the beauty and power of Allah's creation. The Quran mentions, "Do they not look at the sky above them - how We have made it and adorned it, and there are no rifts in it?" (50:6). For example, Hassan took his son to the garden to observe the growth of plants. He explained that every seed grows into a plant by the will of Allah, fostering his son's contemplation of Allah's power over creation. Through these examples, children naturally grow into submitting to the magnificence of Allah.

Instilling Love for the Prophet (peace and blessings of Allah be upon him)

Instilling love for the Prophet (peace and blessings of Allah be upon him) in children is vital and can be done through stories about his life and the lives of his companions. For example, narrating stories of young companions like Usama bin Zaid, who was entrusted with leading an army at a young age, teaches children the values of bravery and devotion to Islam.

A father rewarded his child for memorizing Hadith. By celebrating these efforts, the child's admiration for the Prophet (peace and blessings of Allah be upon him) and his teachings grew.

Similarly, Umm Huda told her children bedtime stories about the Prophet (peace and blessings of Allah be upon him), such as how Allah protected him during the Hijrah to Madinah. These stories strengthened the love of the Prophet (peace and blessings of Allah be upon him) in their hearts and inspired them to follow his example.

Teaching Children Adhkaar

It is essential to introduce children to the Adhkaar (remembrances of Allah) early in life. They should be taught the morning and evening Adhkar and parents should make them say it after their Farj and Asr prayer (which should be done in the mosque in case of boys). Zayd, for example, learned to say "Bismillah" before eating because he constantly heard his parents recite it. One day, during a family picnic, he asked, "What should we say before eating, Mama?" This demonstrated how deeply he had internalized the Adhkaar from his parents' teachings. Another example is a young boy who repeated the Du'a for wearing new clothes after hearing his sister recite it, showing how an Islamic environment naturally shapes a child's behavior.

Practical Tips for Islamic Education at Home

Teach Arabic: Fatimah began teaching her children Arabic through Quran recitation, helping them develop a deeper connection to the language of the Quran.

Teach the Obligations: Parents should also introduce their children to the obligations of Islam early. Although prayer, fasting, and modesty may not be obligatory for children yet, starting early helps build lifelong habits. Bilal, for instance, taught his daughter that prayer is a direct connection to Allah and reminded her that each time she prays, she is conversing with the One who is always near with His knowledge while He is Most High. Read with your child the Book of Tawheed by Sheikh-ul-Islam, Muhammad bin Abdul-Wahhab (Allah have mercy on him).

Superheroes in Islam: Aisha introduced her son to Khalid ibn al-Waleed, the Sword of Allah, as an Islamic hero. This real-life example of bravery and dedication to Islam shifted her son's admiration from fictional superheroes to true Islamic role models.

Distinguishing the Lawful and Unlawful: Ahmad encountered pressure from classmates to join non-Islamic celebrations like Halloween. His parents explained the importance of upholding Islamic principles and guided him to avoid un-Islamic practices.

Communication: Zainab kept open lines of communication with her children about life and religion, regularly discussing the importance of prayer and reminding them that it is their direct link to Allah.

Attachment to the Masjid: Husna encouraged her son to attend the masjid regularly for salah and Islamic classes, rewarding him with small gifts to make the masjid a beloved place.

Connection with the Quran: Ali consistently played Quran recitations for his children and encouraged them to memorize small verses, helping them to see the Quran as a guide and source of light.

Islamic Media: Amina prioritized Islamic media for her children, discussing how Islamic values align with Allah's guidance, whereas secular media often conflicts with these principles.

Umrah: Anas took his children on Umrah, explaining the significance of the rituals and allowing them to experience the spiritual impact of this journey.

Islamic Schools: Sumayyah enrolled her children in an Islamic school, where they were immersed in an environment that nurtured their beliefs and Islamic conduct.

Islamic Routine: Layla created an Islamic routine for her children that included Quran recitation after Fajr prayer and reflecting on Hadith before bed, fostering a lifelong connection to Islamic teachings.

By integrating Islamic education with daily life through stories, real examples, and practical practices, children will grow up with a deep connection to their faith, rooted in a love for Allah and His Messenger (peace and blessings of Allah be upon him), and will embody a strong understanding of Islamic principles in their lives.

Fourteen-year-old Ayyub had been dealing with persistent anxiety, which affected his daily life and his performance at school. His mother was initially distressed, not because she disagreed with the school, but because she was concerned about the impact anxiety was having on Ayyub's well-being. "He's feeling overwhelmed with everything," she said to the school's guidance counselor. "I just want to find a way to help him manage his anxiety so he can focus."

The school suggested therapy, and this time, Ayyub's mother was supportive. She believed that, with proper guidance, Ayyub could overcome his challenges. In the first therapy session, Ayyub and his parents expressed their concerns over his mounting schoolwork and the stress it caused him. Ayyub had fallen behind, and it seemed as though the more he tried to catch up, the more his anxiety increased.

Ayyub's uncle, however, had a different attitude. He constantly remarked, "It's too much pressure for a child to handle. The school isn't being fair; they should make exceptions for him. It's not his fault he's struggling." His uncle's constant emphasis on the difficulty of Ayyub's situation made it seem as if the world was against him. He believed Ayyub couldn't succeed under such stressful conditions.

Ayyub's mother, though, refused to view her son as helpless. She said, "We'll do everything we can to help him, but I believe Ayyub is stronger than this." She knew that part of managing Ayyub's anxiety involved taking care of both his mental and spiritual well-being.

They decided to make some lifestyle changes. Ayyub began to pray five times a day at the mosque. His mother would remind him that seeking Allah's help through prayer would give him the inner peace he needed.

They also made sure that Ayyub got proper rest, particularly after Isha, ensuring he followed the Prophet's (peace and blessings of Allah be upon him) Sunnah of sleeping early and rising for Fajr. His mother made it a point to avoid pressuring him too much about his schoolwork and instead encouraged him to take small steps in managing his anxiety.

At the same time, they started planning for a family Hajj trip. Ayyub's mother believed that such a journey would be spiritually uplifting for him. The idea of Hajj also motivated Ayyub, giving him hope and something to look forward to.

Ayyub started to see changes in his life. Slowly, his grades began to improve. He found that after praying regularly, he felt calmer and more capable of dealing with his schoolwork. His anxiety didn't disappear overnight, but with a focus on prayer, discipline, and trust in Allah, he was learning to manage it better.

His uncle, meanwhile, still held onto the belief that Ayyub needed easier circumstances to succeed. "He shouldn't have to go through all this," his uncle would say. But Ayyub and his mother disagreed. They knew that with faith, effort, and patience, Ayyub was capable of overcoming his anxiety and excelling in his studies.

Over time, Ayyub became more confident. He took control of his studies and embraced the spiritual practices that anchored him. His journey was a reminder that while anxiety is a challenge, with the right mindset, prayer, and support from family, it can be managed. And most importantly, it was a reminder that relying on Allah for guidance and strength can be the greatest source of comfort.

Do You Condone a Victim Mentality in Child Upbringing?

Addressing a victim mentality such as what is shown by Ayyub's uncle in parenting is essential for fostering healthy development and resilience in children. This mindset can influence how parents perceive their circumstances and their child's behavior. Here are some examples illustrating how this mentality manifests:

In Your Personal Life:

- Belief in External Barriers:

Example: Ahmed believes that his inability to advance in his career is solely due to his challenging work environment and lack of opportunities. He feels trapped and unable to change his situation. The Quran in Surah Al-Ankabut (29:69) advises, "And those who strive for Us – We will surely guide them to Our ways." This suggests that effort and perseverance are essential to overcoming obstacles, rather than resigning oneself to external barriers.

- Comparison with Others:

Example: Fatima often compares her modest lifestyle to her more affluent friends and feels she is less fortunate. The Prophet Muhammad (peace be upon him) advised, "Look at those below you and do not look at those above you, for this will make it easier for you to appreciate the blessings of Allah upon you." (Sahih Muslim). This advice encourages gratitude and contentment with one's own situation.

- Belief in Exceptional Problems:

Example: Ibrahim feels his financial struggles are more severe than anyone else's and views them as insurmountable. Allah says in Surah Al-Baqarah (2:286), "Allah does not burden a soul beyond that it can bear." This assures that all difficulties can be managed with patience and effort, countering the belief that one's problems are uniquely insolvable.

- Complaining About Others:

Example: Aisha frequently complains about her colleagues' behavior rather than focusing on improving her own work environment. The

Prophet Muhammad (peace be upon him) said, "Whoever does not thank people has not thanked Allah." (Sunan Abu Dawood). This emphasizes focusing on gratitude and solutions rather than complaints.

- Belief in Unending Misfortune:

Example: Youssef feels that no matter how hard he tries, his life is perpetually unlucky and nothing ever improves. Surah Ash-Sharh (94:5-6) teaches, "For indeed, with hardship [will be] ease. Indeed, with hardship [will be] ease." This verse encourages hope and trust that difficulties are followed by relief.

In Your Parenting Life:

- Misbehavior as Punishment:

Example: Omar sees his child's frequent tantrums as a form of divine punishment for his own past mistakes, which makes him feel victimized. The Prophet Muhammad (peace be upon him) said, "The best of you are those who are best to their families." (Sunan Ibn Majah). This suggests that parenting should involve patience and guidance, rather than viewing challenges as punishments.

- Excusing Failures:

Example: Layla consistently makes excuses for her son's poor academic performance, attributing it to the school system's flaws instead of addressing his personal responsibilities. The Prophet Muhammad (peace be upon him) said, "The strong person is not the one who is good at wrestling, but the strong person is the one who controls himself when he is angry." (Sahih al-Bukhari). This highlights the importance of self-discipline and accountability.

- Feeling Sorry for Your Child:

Example: Yusuf feels excessive pity for his daughter when she faces minor setbacks, leading him to shield her from challenges. The Quran in Surah Al-Hujurat (49:13) teaches, "Indeed, the most noble of you in the sight of Allah is the most righteous of you." This emphasizes the need to nurture self-reliance and strength in children.

- Focusing on Problems Rather Than Solutions:

Example: Zainab spends more time discussing her child's behavioral issues with little focus on finding solutions. The Prophet Muhammad (peace be upon him) said, "Make things easy and do not make them difficult." (Sahih al-Bukhari). Encouraging practical solutions and focusing on positive actions is essential.

- Viewing Your Child as Helpless:

Example: Sarah treats her son as incapable of handling even minor tasks, which affects his confidence and growth. The Quran in Surah Al-Isra (17:70) mentions, "And We have certainly honored the children of Adam." This highlights that every child has inherent dignity and capability that should be nurtured.

Addressing and avoiding a victim mentality in parenting helps align with Islamic principles of resilience, responsibility, and gratitude. By fostering a mindset of effort, self-discipline, and positive action, you can provide effective guidance and support to your child while managing personal challenges.

The Victimhood Culture Makes Everyone a Victim

Historically, victimhood was closely associated with severe injustices, such as experiencing violent crimes or severe oppression. However, in today's "victimhood culture," individuals sometimes perceive themselves as victims over relatively minor issues. This shift is seen when people consider themselves victims due to less significant problems, such as fluctuations in the housing market or minor inconveniences.

In Islam, the approach to dealing with grievances is guided by wisdom and patience. Allah instructs in Surah Al-Ankabut (29:69), "And those who strive for Us – We will surely guide them to Our ways." This verse encourages Muslims to strive for perseverance and patience rather than adopting a victim mentality.

Consider the case of Ahmed, a young Muslim student facing challenges at school. Ahmed is a bright student, but he recently failed a class project, was overlooked for a school award, and was benched during a sports event. In a culture that promotes a victim mentality, Ahmed might start seeing these setbacks as deliberate obstacles placed by others to hinder his success. He might begin to think that his failures are due to unfair treatment rather than recognizing these as opportunities for growth and improvement.

Islamic teachings emphasize resilience and personal responsibility. The Prophet Muhammad (peace be upon him) said, "The strong person is not the one who is good at wrestling, but the strong person is the one who controls himself when he is angry." (Sahih al-Bukhari). This Hadith underscores the importance of emotional strength and self-discipline in facing challenges. Ahmed is encouraged to respond to his setbacks with patience and perseverance, reflecting the resilience shown by the Companions of the Prophet Muhammad (peace be upon him), such as Bilal ibn Rabah (may Allah be pleased with him). Despite facing severe torture for his faith, Bilal (may Allah be pleased with him) remained steadfast and patient, eventually becoming a respected and honored figure in Islam.

Raising a mentally resilient child like Ahmed in a culture that promotes victimhood involves instilling values of patience and self-discipline. Islamic teachings, illustrated by the story of Prophet Ayoub (peace be upon him), who endured great suffering with unwavering patience and faith, provide a profound example of maintaining steadfastness and gratitude in the face of trials. By embracing these teachings, Ahmed can navigate his challenges with resilience and a positive mindset.

A Victim Mentality Can Be Inherited

In a devout Islamic household, parents play a crucial role in shaping their children's spiritual and emotional development. When parents, due to their own past experiences, internalize a victim mentality, they may unknowingly pass this mindset on to their children. Even without explicitly labeling themselves as victims, their attitudes and behaviors can subtly communicate helplessness, with messages like, "You won't succeed, so don't even try." This negative mindset stifles the child's potential and contradicts core Islamic values such as tawakkul (reliance on Allah), sabr (patience), and perseverance in overcoming life's challenges.

Islam teaches that hardships are part of Allah's divine plan to test and strengthen the believers. In Surah Al-Baqarah (2:286), Allah reminds us: "Allah does not burden a soul beyond that it can bear." This verse assures Muslims that Allah provides each person with the capacity to handle their challenges, allowing them to draw closer to Him. Parents who embody this Islamic perspective encourage their children to view difficulties as opportunities for spiritual growth, rather than insurmountable obstacles.

Take Yasir, a boy whose mother, Aisha, faced severe financial difficulties and lacked emotional support throughout her life. Aisha internalized a feeling of powerlessness, believing that no matter what she did, she was doomed to fail. This mentality influenced how she raised Yasir. Although Aisha never called herself a victim, her frequent statements like, "Why does everything go wrong for us?" conveyed a sense of defeatism.

When Yasir struggled in school, whether academically or socially, he absorbed his mother's negativity. Instead of viewing these challenges as part of life's tests from Allah, Yasir began to see failure as inevitable. This mindset directly contradicted the teachings of the Prophet Muhammad (peace be upon him), who said: "Strive for that which benefits you, seek help from Allah, and do not give up." (Sahih Muslim). Had Aisha instilled an Islamic mindset grounded in trust in Allah, Yasir could have learned perseverance and hope instead of resignation.

Examples of Instilling a Victim Mentality

Even in a religious Muslim household, certain behaviors may inadvertently nurture a victim mentality in children:

1. Role-modeling a victim mentality: A parent who regularly expresses feelings of despair by saying things like, "Why do bad things always happen to me?" unknowingly teaches their child a sense of helplessness. However, Islam encourages believers to place their trust in Allah. In Surah Ar-Ra'd (13:11), Allah says: "Indeed, Allah will not change the condition of a people until they change what is in themselves." This highlights the importance of taking positive action and trusting Allah's wisdom.

Example: During the time of the Prophet Muhammad (peace be upon him), a woman who had lost her son was weeping uncontrollably at his grave. The Prophet (peace be upon him) approached her and reminded her to be patient and seek reward from Allah. (Sahih Bukhari). This incident teaches that even in the face of great sorrow, patience and trust in Allah are the best responses, rather than despair.

2. Feeling sorry for your child: Some parents, out of love, may feel pity for their child's difficulties, such as a disability or trauma. However, even unspoken pity may give the child a sense of being inherently

disadvantaged. Islam promotes hope, encouraging resilience and belief in Allah's justice. In Surah Ash-Sharh (94:6), Allah reassures believers: "Indeed, with hardship comes ease."

When a blind man came to the Prophet (peace be upon him) seeking guidance, the Prophet treated him with respect and empowered him to continue worshipping Allah sincerely. This reflects how Islam values every individual's potential, focusing on their strengths rather than their limitations.

3. Underestimating a child's capabilities: Parents who emphasize their child's weaknesses—whether due to a physical or cognitive condition—can cultivate a sense of helplessness in them. Islam, on the other hand, encourages believers to work on their strengths and ask Allah for help where they are weak. The Prophet Muhammad (peace be upon him) stressed the importance of utilizing one's talents for good while relying on Allah for support in areas of difficulty.

During the Prophet's time, Abdullah ibn Umm Maktum (may Allah be pleased with him), who was blind, was given the honorable role of calling the Adhan (call to prayer). This example shows that even with disabilities, believers can contribute meaningfully to society.

4. Refusing to let a child struggle: Although it is difficult for parents to watch their children face adversity, constantly shielding them from difficulties deprives them of the opportunity to develop resilience. In Islam, facing adversity with patience and faith in Allah brings immense spiritual reward. Allowing children to confront their struggles helps build their character and strengthens their trust in Allah.

Example: The story of the Prophet Musa (peace be upon him) illustrates how facing hardships fosters spiritual growth. After fleeing from Pharaoh's tyranny, Musa (peace be upon him) faced hunger, thirst, and fear, but remained firm in his reliance on Allah. His perseverance was rewarded with safety, guidance, and eventually, leadership. This teaches that hardships are a means to strengthen one's faith and character.

Case History: Ayyub and His Struggles

Ayyub's uncle, out of love and concern for his anxiety, often intervened to ease his difficulties. Whether by completing his homework for him or shielding him from uncomfortable social interactions, he unintentionally reinforced the idea that Ayyub was incapable of managing life's challenges on his own.

However, Islam views adversity as an essential part of one's spiritual development. The story of Prophet Ayyub (peace be upon him) serves as a timeless example of patience during severe trials. Despite his extreme physical and emotional suffering, Prophet Ayyub remained steadfast in his trust in Allah. As mentioned in Surah Saad (38:44): "Indeed, We found him patient, an excellent servant. Indeed, he was one repeatedly turning back [to Allah]."

The Consequences of a Victim Mentality: Zainab's Story

Zainab experienced bullying as a child, which left emotional scars that she carried into adulthood. Fearing her children would face the same, she would often tell them, "Other children are cruel," and recount her own painful experiences. This created a sense of helplessness in her children, making them anxious and withdrawn.

From an Islamic perspective, living with fear and despair contradicts the teachings of perseverance and trust in Allah. In Surah Al-Baqarah (2:286), Allah reminds us that He does not burden any soul beyond its capacity. Believers are taught to turn to Allah in times of hardship, seeking His guidance and strength rather than allowing fear to dictate their lives. Had Zainab instilled these principles in her children, she could have fostered resilience and confidence in them, allowing them to face life's challenges with faith in Allah's wisdom.

Islamically, fostering a victim mentality contradicts the values of resilience, patience, and reliance on Allah. Parents hold a vital responsibility to model positive attitudes, trust in Allah's plan, and the courage to face adversity with patience. By teaching children to approach life's trials with faith and strength, parents help them grow into resilient, empowered individuals who trust in Allah, rather than seeing themselves as powerless victims.

Breaking the Cycle of a Victim Mentality

When children adopt a victim mentality, it deeply affects their thoughts and behavior. A child who feels powerless might think, "There is nothing I can do to change this situation." This mindset leads to inaction, passivity, and a sense of helplessness. From an Islamic perspective, however, such a mentality contradicts the principles of sabr (patience), tawakkul (reliance on Allah), and ihsan (striving for excellence) that Allah and His Messenger (peace and blessings be upon him) have commanded us to embody.

The Quran and the Sunnah guide us that, no matter the circumstances, a believer is never truly powerless. Take the example of Prophet Yusuf (peace be upon him). In Surah Yusuf, Allah describes the many trials Yusuf faced, including being thrown into a well by his brothers, sold into slavery, falsely accused, and imprisoned. Despite these severe trials, Yusuf did not adopt a victim mentality. He exhibited remarkable patience and continued to place his trust in Allah. His unwavering faith led to his eventual rise to power and reunion with his family. As Allah mentions in the Quran: "Indeed, he who fears Allah and is patient, then surely Allah does not allow the reward of the righteous to be lost." (Surah Yusuf, 12:90). This story exemplifies how sabr and tawakkul lead to Allah's divine assistance and success, even in the most challenging situations.

Fatimah, a young girl who faced persistent bullying at school. Instead of falling into despair, her parents reminded her of Prophet Yusuf's story. They explained that, just as Yusuf faced hardship but eventually triumphed through patience and reliance on Allah, she too could overcome her difficulties. Fatimah began making dua' regularly, asking Allah for strength and guidance, while also engaging in her salah with mindfulness (khushu'), seeking Allah's protection and support. Over time, she developed the confidence to stand up to her bullies, sought help from her teachers, and began to trust that Allah's plan for her was always filled with wisdom, even when things seemed difficult.

In my work with Muslim youth, I have often encountered young people struggling with feelings of helplessness. For example, when students fall behind in their studies or face difficulties with friends, they sometimes start believing that they are incapable of improving their situation. This form of learned helplessness—where a person believes they are unable to influence their circumstances—can weaken their connection to Allah and lead them to neglect the essential effort and reliance on Allah that Islam emphasizes.

An insightful lesson comes from a well-known psychological study conducted by Martin Seligman in 1967, which was not done by Islamic principles and tortured the creation of Allah, but this study illustrates the dangers of internalizing helplessness. In the study, dogs were subjected to electric shocks; one group could stop the shocks by pressing a lever, while the other group had no control. Later, when both groups were placed in an environment where they could easily escape the shocks, only the dogs who had previously been able to control their circumstances sought to escape. The others, having internalized helplessness, remained passive and did not even try to escape. While this study involves animals and differs from Islamic principles, it sheds light on a similar phenomenon in humans. People who believe they are powerless often give up, even when solutions are within reach.

In contrast, Islam teaches us to seek Allah's help while also taking action to improve our situation. The Prophet Muhammad (peace and blessings be upon him) embodied this principle. He faced numerous hardships—such as the loss of his beloved wife Khadijah (may Allah be pleased with her), the death of his uncle Abu Talib, and severe persecution from the Quraysh. Yet, he never adopted a victim mentality. Instead, he constantly turned to Allah through dua' and striving for solutions. During the Battle of Badr, for example, the Muslims were outnumbered and faced a formidable enemy. Yet, they placed their trust in Allah, fought with courage, and achieved victory through Allah's help. This victory teaches us that when we rely on Allah and exert effort, Allah's assistance will come, no matter how overwhelming the odds may seem (Surah Al-Imran, 3:123).

What to Do Instead

Let's consider another case: Abdullah, a young boy struggling with anxiety. Initially, his parents saw his condition as something outside of their control. However, after deepening their understanding of Islamic teachings, they realized that Abdullah's anxiety could be managed through reliance on Allah and the application of Islamic practices. His parents taught him to make dua' and practice khushu' (mindfulness and humility) during his salah, reminding him to focus on his connection with Allah. Abdullah began to see his anxiety not as an insurmountable obstacle but as a test from Allah. By exercising patience and faith, using the tools provided by Allah, Abdullah slowly gained control over his anxiety and found peace in turning to Allah.

Another case involves Omar, a student who was falling behind in his studies. He began to believe that he could never catch up and fell into despair. His teacher noticed his struggles and reminded him of the story of Prophet Musa (peace be upon him) when he faced Pharaoh, the most powerful ruler of his time, armed with nothing but his faith in Allah and reliance on His plan. The teacher encouraged Omar to make dua' for success and to organize his time more efficiently. Omar began to approach his studies with renewed confidence, inspired by Musa's unwavering trust in Allah. Over time, his grades improved, and his belief in himself and his trust in Allah were restored, just as Prophet Musa's trust in Allah led to miraculous victories over Pharaoh.

Had Abdullah's and Omar's parents not embraced an Islamic approach, their children might have grown up internalizing a sense of helplessness. Instead, their families understood that Islam offers solutions to every difficulty. The Prophet Muhammad (peace and blessings be upon him) said, "Strive for that which benefits you, seek help from Allah, and do not be helpless." (Sahih Muslim). This hadith emphasizes the balance between taking proactive steps and maintaining complete reliance on Allah.

Islam provides countless examples of resilience and patience. One of the most powerful is the story of Prophet Ayub (peace be upon him), who endured extreme hardship when Allah tested him by taking away his wealth, children, and health. Despite these overwhelming trials, Ayub never complained and continued to worship Allah with steadfast faith. His devotion was ultimately rewarded when Allah restored his health and blessed him with more than he had before. As mentioned in Surah Sad (38:44), Allah emphasizes that Ayub was patient and remained devoted to Him throughout his trial, teaching us that with patience and trust in Allah, relief and reward will come.

In modern psychology, Carol Dweck's concept of a growth mindset is another powerful tool to combat a victim mentality. Dweck's research emphasizes that individuals who believe that their abilities can be developed through dedication and hard work are more likely to overcome challenges and thrive. This mindset aligns with Islamic teachings, where perseverance (sabr) and effort (jihad an-nafs) are highly valued. By adopting a growth mindset, a child who might initially feel overwhelmed by difficulties can shift their thinking towards viewing challenges as opportunities for growth, similar to how Islam teaches that trials are a means of purification and reward from Allah.

When young Muslims face hardships, reminding them of Allah's wisdom and the potential for spiritual growth can shift their perspective from victimhood to resilience.

As parents or guardians, it is important to assess whether we unintentionally reinforce a victim mentality in our children. Are we emphasizing their struggles without encouraging them to rely on Allah and seek practical solutions? Are we making them feel powerless instead of reminding them that, with Allah's help, they have the strength to overcome life's challenges?

Help your child recognize that they are resilient and capable by fostering their trust in Allah and their ability to take action. Encourage them to adopt tawakkul—trust in Allah—while also putting in the necessary effort. Remind them of the examples of the Prophet Muhammad (peace and blessings be upon him), the Sahabah, and other prophets who faced tremendous adversity but remained hopeful in Allah's mercy and worked to improve their situations.

Islam teaches us that hardships are a test and a means for purification and elevation in the sight of Allah. Allah says in Surah Al-Baqarah (2:286): "Allah does not burden a soul beyond that it can bear." Every trial is within our capacity to endure, with Allah's help. By fostering resilience, sabr, and reliance on Allah, we can break the cycle of victimhood and empower ourselves and our children to face life's challenges with unwavering trust in Allah.

Be a Good Role Model

A victim mentality stands in stark contrast to the Islamic principle of tawakkul (reliance on Allah). By focusing solely on hardships and not seeking solutions, a parent inadvertently teaches children a sense of helplessness when facing challenges. This mindset can foster a belief that external forces dictate their destiny, rather than embracing the Islamic belief that everything happens by Allah's decree, and we are responsible for how we respond.

Take the story of Zainab, a single mother who went through a difficult divorce. She frequently expressed frustration, saying things like, "Life is so unfair," or "I can't catch a break." Over time, her son, Abdullah, began to absorb this mindset, believing that his struggles were beyond his control. However, Zainab realized the effect this was having on Abdullah and decided to shift her approach. She began emphasizing tawakkul, reminding her son of the verse, "Allah does not burden a soul beyond what it can bear" (Surah Al-Baqarah, 2:286). Zainab turned to prayer and proactive efforts to improve their situation, modeling for Abdullah that even in hardship, a believer must rely on Allah and take action.

From a psychological perspective, Martin Seligman, in his work on learned optimism, underscores that shifting from a victim mindset to a proactive one significantly impacts well-being. Just as Zainab changed her approach, she instilled resilience in Abdullah, helping him develop a mindset aligned with Islamic teachings of tawakkul and action.

In Islamic history, we find similar lessons in the life of the Prophet Muhammad (peace and blessings be upon him). During the Meccan boycott of the Muslims, the Prophet and his companions faced severe hardship. However, he remained patient and steadfast, trusting Allah's plan. This resilience allowed them to persevere until Allah granted them relief. Like the Prophet, we must teach our children resilience through patience and reliance on Allah, guiding them to see adversity as part of the divine test, as mentioned in the Quran: "And We will surely test you with something of fear and hunger and a loss of wealth and lives and fruits, but give good tidings to the patient" (Surah Al-Baqarah, 2:155).

Be positive: How you speak about your circumstances profoundly influences your child's perception of life. For example, Mariam, a working mother, often complained about financial difficulties. Her daughter, Aisha, began to view life as unfair, adopting a similar negative mindset. Inspired by listening to scholars such as Shaykh Saleh Al-Fawzan, Mariam decided to shift her perspective. She began expressing gratitude for blessings like health and sustenance, and over time, Aisha's outlook improved as well. Allah says in the Quran, "And whoever fears Allah—He will make for him a way out and will provide for him from where he does not expect" (Surah At-Talaq, 65:2-3). By focusing on gratitude and hope, Mariam reshaped Aisha's perspective, reinforcing that reliance on Allah should outweigh despair.

Psychological research also supports this approach. Dr. Barbara Fredrickson's "Broaden-and-Build" theory of positive emotions suggests that cultivating positive emotions, such as gratitude, broadens one's thinking and leads to greater resilience over time. This can be tied to the Islamic concept of shukr (gratitude) and how expressing it can bring about Allah's blessings, which has been mentioned in Surah Ibrahim, "If you are grateful, I will surely increase you [in favor]" (Surah Ibrahim, 14:7).

Resist venting: Excessive venting can create a negative cycle, deepening the sense of helplessness. Islam encourages self-control and turning to Allah for solace. The Prophet Muhammad (peace and blessings be upon him) demonstrated this during some of the hardest moments of his life. When he lost his beloved wife Khadijah and his uncle Abu Talib, he did not complain but sought refuge in prayer and dhikr (remembrance of Allah).

Similarly, Sarah, a woman who lost her job, initially vented her frustrations to friends, which only exacerbated her feelings of hopelessness. She was inspired by the importance of patience and du'a (supplication). Turning to dhikr and du'a, Sarah found peace, allowing her to remain positive and model reliance on Allah for her children. This reflects the Quranic wisdom that with every hardship comes ease (Surah Ash-Sharh, 94:6).

In self-help psychology, Dr. Brené Brown emphasizes in her research on vulnerability that while it's important to express emotions, overindulgence in venting can lead to further emotional exhaustion. Instead, turning to solutions—much like Sarah did through du'a—fosters resilience and healing.

Create positive change: Islam encourages believers to be agents of good in society. For example, Bilal, a father, and his son Yusuf participated in a neighborhood cleanup initiative, inspired by the saying of the Prophet Muhammad (peace and blessings be upon him), "The best of people are those who are most beneficial to others". This act of charity helped Yusuf understand that Muslims have a responsibility to contribute positively to their community. Bilal's approach emphasizes the importance of engaging in good deeds that benefit others and bring fulfillment.

From a psychological standpoint, helping others has been proven to reduce stress and promote happiness. In his book Give and Take, Adam Grant discusses how giving can lead to greater success and well-being, echoing the Islamic teaching that charity is a means of attaining Allah's blessings.

Be assertive: Islam teaches us to seek justice with dignity and patience. Caliph Umar ibn al-Khattab (may Allah be pleased with him) is a prime example of this. He was known for ensuring fairness and justice for the weak while maintaining humility. In a similar vein, Faiz felt wronged by his teacher, and his father, Ali, encouraged him to respectfully address the issue. Ali explained that Islam teaches us to seek justice with patience and dignity. This lesson aligns with the principles found in Islam, emphasizing patience, respect, and maintaining one's dignity when addressing grievances.

Assertiveness is also encouraged in self-help psychology. Dr. Randy Paterson, in his book The Assertiveness Workbook, teaches that assertiveness is about standing up for oneself in a manner that respects the rights of others, which mirrors the Islamic principle of justice with decorum.

Go After the Good

Fatimah's daughter, Amina, often focused on the negative aspects of her school day, complaining about noisy classmates or strict rules. Initially, Fatimah sympathized with her, unintentionally reinforcing the negative focus. However, later Fatimah began to redirect Amina's attention by asking, "What was something good that happened today?" This subtle shift in perspective allowed Amina to focus on positive moments, helping her to appreciate the blessings in her life.

The Prophet Muhammad (peace and blessings be upon him) similarly emphasized the importance of focusing on positivity. During the Battle of the Trench, even in the face of overwhelming odds, the Prophet kept the spirits of his companions high by reminding them of Allah's aid and promises of future success. This positive outlook was key in helping them endure adversity.

Similarly, Ahmad, a boy who struggled with his studies, frequently complained about the difficulty of his subjects. His parents began to acknowledge his efforts, saying, "Alhamdulillah, you completed your homework today, that's progress!" This small acknowledgment helped Ahmad realize that perseverance, combined with tawakkul, leads to success. His parents were following the guidance of the Prophet Muhammad (peace and blessings be upon him), who said, "Wondrous is the affair of the believer, for there is good for him in every matter... If he is happy, he thanks Allah, and if he is harmed, he shows patience" (Sahih Muslim). This encouragement to focus on the good in every situation fosters resilience and helps children understand that hardships, too, are part of Allah's plan and will eventually lead to ease.

Empowering Your Child by Focusing on What They Can Control

As a devout Muslim parent, guiding your child to focus on what they can control is a fundamental part of fostering resilience, patience, and reliance on Allah (the Most High). Life presents various challenges—whether it's a personal struggle like disliking school or a more difficult situation like the effects of war. It is natural to feel overwhelmed by what seems beyond our control, but Islam teaches that while we cannot control every external situation, we can always choose how to respond. This lesson helps children learn empowerment through faith, understanding that their actions and attitudes are within their grasp, and they are responsible before Allah for those choices.

Allah says in the Quran: "Indeed, Allah will not change the condition of a people until they change what is in themselves." (Surah Ar-Ra'd, 13:11). This verse reminds us that inner transformation starts with our own choices—our thoughts, attitudes, and actions. Empowering your child with this understanding helps them approach life's trials with patience and purpose, seeking to change what they can within themselves.

The "Circle of Control" Concept

One useful tool for teaching children this mindset is the concept of the "Circle of Control," commonly used in self-help and psychology. This concept highlights the importance of distinguishing between what is within our control—our actions, thoughts, and attitudes—and what is beyond our control, like the actions of others or unforeseen events. Encouraging your child to focus on their own "circle of control" helps reduce feelings of helplessness and builds confidence. This aligns perfectly with Islamic teachings on tawakkul (trust in Allah) and sabr (patience), emphasizing that while we take positive actions, we trust the outcome to Allah.

An excellent example from Islamic history is the story of Prophet Yusuf (peace be upon him). Betrayed by his own brothers and sold into slavery, Yusuf had no control over these external circumstances. Yet, what makes his story inspiring is how he chose to respond. Instead of falling into despair or anger, Yusuf maintained his patience and placed his trust in Allah. His steadfastness is rewarded when he is eventually elevated to a position of power and authority, where justice is served. For a child who feels victimized, such as being bullied at school, the story of Yusuf teaches that while they may not control others' actions, they can always control their own responses by staying patient, turning to Allah, informing the parents and teachers, and knowing that justice belongs to Him.

The Battle of Uhud is another profound example from Islamic history. The Muslims faced a severe setback after initial victory due to an error. However, the Prophet Muhammad (peace and blessings be upon him) remained calm and steadfast, despite the adversity. He focused on what he could control—encouraging his companions to remain patient and continue to trust in Allah's wisdom. This historical lesson illustrates for your child that even when the outcome of a situation does not turn out as expected, staying patient, maintaining reliance on Allah, and adjusting one's actions within their control are key to success.

The story of Prophet Ayyub (peace be upon him) offers a perfect example of resilience in the face of extreme hardship. Struck with severe illness for years, Ayyub could not control his health, but he remained steadfast in his faith, constantly turning to Allah in supplication. Eventually, Allah rewarded him for his patience with healing and restoration. Teaching your child this example helps them understand that while we cannot always control our physical state or external events, our spiritual response remains in our control. Like Ayyub, we can choose patience, prayer, and trust in Allah's plan, even in adversity.

Ahmad, a young boy who undergoes frequent medical procedures, struggled with the pain and anxiety associated with them. His parents introduced Islamic coping strategies such as reciting Quranic verses, making du'a, and practicing mindfulness techniques like deep breathing. For example, Ahmad recites "So verily, with the hardship, there is relief" (Surah Ash-Sharh, 94:6) when he feels anxious before a medical procedure. These practices help him regain a sense of control over his emotions and remind him that his trials are a test from Allah, with relief eventually following. This approach helps children focus on their inner control while trusting in Allah's greater wisdom.

Ibn Al-Qayyim, in his famous works, emphasized the virtue of sabr (patience) as one of the highest forms of worship. He wrote extensively about how trials are a means of purification for the believer, and enduring them with patience elevates one's status before Allah. Teaching your child from these Islamic teachings reinforces that while they may not be able to change every situation, their choice to remain patient and steadfast can bring them closer to Allah and lead to greater rewards.

Amina is facing bullying at school and feels powerless to stop her peers' hurtful behavior. Her parents remind her that although she cannot control their actions, she can control how she responds. Amina decides to make du'a, asking Allah for strength and protection, and she practices patience. Additionally, she speaks to a teacher, taking positive steps to protect herself.

Teaching Your Child to Take Control through Positive Actions

Empowering your child to focus on what they can control helps nurture their emotional resilience and spiritual growth. The Prophet Muhammad (peace and blessings be upon him) said, "Strive for that which will benefit you, seek help from Allah, and do not give up." (Sahih Muslim). Encourage your child to act on what they can control, seek Allah's assistance through prayer, and leave what they cannot control in Allah's hands.

Ask your child questions such as:

- What can you control in this situation?

- What choices are available to you?

- What attitude will you choose, knowing Allah rewards patience and perseverance?

By guiding your child in this manner, you help them develop emotional resilience, self-awareness, and stronger faith. Remind them that every trial is an opportunity for purification, and by choosing patience and gratitude, they will attain rewards in this life and the hereafter. The hadith "Wondrous is the affair of the believer, for there is good for him in every matter... If he is harmed, he shows patience, and that is good for him" (Sahih Muslim) encapsulates the essence of this teaching.

Differentiating Between Negative and True Thoughts

As devout Muslim parents, it is essential to teach your child that not all thoughts reflect the truth. In Islam, we are taught to guard our hearts and minds against harmful thoughts and whispers (waswasa) that can lead us away from trusting in Allah and His wisdom. For instance, when your child has had a difficult day or feels down, their thoughts may lean toward negativity, worsening their mood and leading them to believe they are helpless victims. Allah, the Most High, reminds us in the Quran: "Indeed, the soul is inclined to evil, except those upon whom my Lord has mercy." (Surah Yusuf, 12:53). This serves as a reminder that unchecked thoughts can lead to misunderstanding our situation, resulting in emotional and spiritual harm.

To help your child navigate such challenges, it is important to teach them to recognize cognitive distortions and align their thoughts with Islamic teachings.

Here's how you can apply this model to help your child differentiate between negative and true thoughts:

Blaming Everyone Else

One common distortion involves blaming others for problems. For example, your child might say, "My teacher never tells us what to study for tests, so I always get bad grades." Islam teaches personal responsibility, as each individual is accountable before Allah for their actions. Encourage your child to take responsibility for their efforts. Remind them of the Hadith: "The strong one is not the one who overpowers others in wrestling, but the strong one is the one who controls himself when he is angry." (Sahih Bukhari).

If your son, Ahmed, blames his teacher for his poor grades, ask him, "Is it really all your teacher's fault? Could you have studied harder?" Help him see that while the teacher may have a role, Ahmed also has control over his efforts, including seeking Allah's help through du'a and consistent work.

If Ahmed fails at a sports competition and blames his coach for not training him well, remind him of how the Prophet Muhammad (peace and blessings be upon him) took personal responsibility for the decisions made by his companions during the Battle of Uhud. Instead of blaming external factors, they acknowledged their mistake of abandoning their posts, sought forgiveness from Allah, and learned from it.

Looking for the Bad News

When someone develops a victim mentality, they may ignore the positive and focus solely on the negative. For instance, instead of appreciating that they got to swim, your child might say, "It was horrible! It started raining, and we had to come home early." Remind them of the Quranic command to be grateful: "If you are grateful, I will certainly give you more." (Surah Ibrahim, 14:7). Acknowledging blessings, even during tough times, opens the door to more.

When your daughter, Amina, complains that the swimming trip was ruined by rain, ask her, "Did you enjoy swimming before it rained? Wasn't that a good part of the day?" Encourage her to recognize the positives, helping her develop gratitude toward Allah for the good moments.

Suppose your daughter, Amina, focuses on how she performed poorly in one subject at school despite excelling in all the others. Remind her that even the Prophet Muhammad (peace and blessings be upon him) went through many trials, such as the boycott by the Quraysh, where they faced extreme difficulties. However, he remained hopeful and continued to find positives in situations, such as the unity it brought to the Muslim community.

Unhappy Guessing

A victim mentality often leads to pessimistic predictions, such as "I'm going to fail my test tomorrow," which may cause a child to give up trying altogether. Islam encourages hope and reliance on Allah alongside necessary effort. Allah says: "And whoever relies upon Allah – then He is sufficient for him." (Surah At-Talaq, 65:3). Teach your child to study, make du'a, and trust Allah's help.

If your daughter, Fatima, says she's going to fail her test, ask her, "What can you do to prevent that from happening?" Encourage her to study as much as possible, make du'a, and trust that Allah will guide her to success.

Suppose Fatima is nervous about giving a presentation and says, "I'll probably forget everything and mess up." Remind her of how Prophet Musa (peace be upon him) felt nervous about confronting Pharaoh. He prayed to Allah for ease and success in his task, saying, "My Lord, expand for me my chest, and ease for me my task." (Surah Ta-Ha, 20:25-26). Teach her that just as Musa (peace be upon him) trusted in Allah and succeeded, she too can pray and rely on Allah's help while preparing diligently.

Exaggerated Negativity

Sometimes, children's imaginations exaggerate problems when they are upset. For instance, your child may say, "Everyone in the whole school is mad at me!" after an argument with a couple of friends. Help them see that their thoughts are exaggerated, and guide them to seek the truth. Islam warns against exaggeration.

When your son, Abdullah, says, "Everyone is mad at me," ask him, "What about your friend Omar? Didn't you two have lunch together yesterday?" Help him find exceptions to counter exaggerated negativity.

Suppose Abdullah exaggerates after losing a soccer game, saying, "I'm the worst player on the team." Guide Abdullah to understand that one setback does not define him, and that with patience and trust in Allah, things can improve.

Encourage Thoughtful Reflection

When your child feels like everything is going wrong, help them pause and reflect. Ask them, "Is this a negative thought or a true thought?" Teach them to recognize overly negative thoughts and replace them with more balanced and positive ones. Remind them of Allah's wisdom, even when circumstances seem difficult, as He promises: "Verily, with hardship comes ease." (Surah Ash-Sharh, 94:6).

If your child says, "Nothing good ever happens to me," ask them to recall moments of ease after hardships. By reflecting on Allah's support during past struggles, they can be reminded of His constant guidance.

Suppose your child becomes upset because they feel left out by their peers. Encourage them to reflect on times when Allah brought them ease after facing similar hardships. For instance, if they once had difficulty making friends but later found a supportive group, remind them of that experience and of Allah's promise in the Quran: "And whoever fears Allah – He will make for him a way out and provide for him from where he does not expect." (Surah At-Talaq, 65:2-3).

By encouraging your child to pause and reflect on their blessings and past experiences, you help them develop resilience, patience, and a trust that Allah will guide them through all difficulties.

Chapter 2

Ethical education, from an Islamic perspective, involves raising children with a strong foundation of righteous moral principles and Islamic values. This ensures that children grow up as productive members of the Ummah, positively contributing to society while maintaining a strong connection to their faith. The importance of this is illustrated in the Quran, where Allah says: "O you who have believed, protect yourselves and your families from a Fire whose fuel is people and stones..." (Surah At-Tahrim, 66:6). This verse highlights the parental responsibility of safeguarding their families from Hellfire by teaching them Islamic ethics and morals.

When children are raised with a firm belief in Allah, they naturally incline toward moral behavior and good conduct. This reflects the innate disposition toward goodness that Allah has placed within every human being, as He says: "So set your face toward the religion, inclining to truth, [Adhere to] the fitrah of Allah upon which He has created [all] people..." (Surah Ar-Rum, 30:30). Parents who fail to nurture this disposition by neglecting Islamic teachings may face disappointment as their children stray from the path of righteousness. This concept is reinforced by the Hadith: "Every child is born upon the fitrah, but his parents make him a Jew or a Christian or a Magian..." (Bukhari).

Prophet Muhammad (peace and blessings of Allah be upon him) emphasized the responsibility of parents in instilling Islamic values. He said: "There is no gift that a father gives his child better than good manners" (Tirmidhi). Parents must guide their children to be honest, truthful, and selfless, avoiding immoral behaviors such as abuse and insults. They should teach respect for elders, generosity toward neighbors, care for the poor and orphans, and compassion for the less fortunate.

Moral Values to Teach Our Children

1. Respect:

Respect is fundamental in Islam. Teaching children to respect others, especially their elders and authority figures, fosters self-discipline and patience. The Prophet (peace and blessings of Allah be upon him) demonstrated this principle by standing to greet his daughter Fatimah, showing respect and affection. He said: "He is not one of us who does not show mercy to our young ones and respect to our elders." (Tirmidhi).

Zayd, a respectful boy, follows his parents' teachings and patiently waits his turn to speak in class. When his friend loses his temper and speaks rudely to the teacher, Zayd gently reminds him of the Hadith his parents taught him about showing mercy and respect.

In "The 7 Habits of Highly Effective People" by Stephen Covey, the value of respect is central to personal leadership and relationships. The Prophet (peace and blessings of Allah be upon him)'s teachings reinforce this, encouraging Muslims to treat others with dignity, building a character based on Islamic values and universal principles.

2. Humility:

Humility in Islam involves recognizing one's weaknesses and seeking Allah's help. The Quran praises the humble, saying: "And the servants of the Most Merciful are those who walk upon the earth easily..." (Surah Al-Furqan, 25:63). Prophet Musa's humility is exemplified when he sought Allah's help in facing Pharaoh's tyranny (Surah Ta-Ha, 20:25-28).

Aisha excels in her studies but remains humble, acknowledging Allah's blessings. When a classmate struggles, she offers help without arrogance, understanding that her success is a gift from Allah.

This mirrors the lessons from "The Road Less Traveled" by M. Scott Peck, where humility and self-discipline are emphasized as essential to personal growth, aligning with Islamic values of humility and grace.

3. Responsibility:

Instilling responsibility from a young age shapes character. Whether in schoolwork, chores, or prayer, responsibility develops discipline and prepares children for future challenges. The story of Abdullah ibn Umar, who sought to take responsibility as a youth, highlights this value.

Fatimah wakes up for Fajr, completes her homework, and helps with household chores without reminders, reflecting the responsibility her parents instilled in her.

4. Obedience:

Obedience to Allah, His Messenger (peace and blessings of Allah be upon him), and parents is critical. The Quran states: "And your Lord has decreed that you not worship except Him, and to parents, good treatment." (Surah Al-Isra, 17:23). The story of Prophet Ismail's obedience to Ibrahim demonstrates perfect submission to Allah (Surah As-Saffat, 37:102-107).

Bilal promptly accompanies his father to the masjid, reflecting the value of obedience taught by his parents and the story of Prophet Ismail.

---

5. POLITENESS:

Islam promotes politeness and good manners. The Prophet (peace and blessings of Allah be upon him) said: "The most beloved of you to me are those who have the best character." (Bukhari).

Maryam diffuses a tense situation at school with her kindness, responding politely when a classmate rudely interrupts her.

This relates to the teachings in Dale Carnegie's "How to Win Friends and Influence People," which highlights the power of courtesy and respect—qualities deeply embedded in Islamic ethics.

6. Honesty:

Honesty is a core value in Islam. The Quran commands believers to stand for justice, even against themselves (Surah An-Nisa, 4:135). The story of Prophet Yusuf and his brothers exemplifies how truth triumphs over deception (Surah Yusuf, 12).

Ahmad confesses to breaking a vase, remembering the story of Prophet Yusuf and the importance of honesty, which earns him his parents' forgiveness.

---

7. FRIENDLINESS:

Islam encourages kindness and friendliness, with even a smile considered charity.

Hasan warmly welcomes a new student in his class, sharing his lunch and showing the friendly nature encouraged in Islam.

8. Bravery:

Bravery in Islam includes both physical and moral courage. The story of Usama bin Zayd, who led an army at 18, illustrates bravery.

Hajar stands up for a classmate being bullied, inspired by Islamic teachings on bravery and justice.

9. Standing for Justice:

Justice is a central Islamic value. The Quran commands believers to always stand for what is right (Surah An-Nisa, 4:135).

Omar speaks out when he witnesses a friend being treated unfairly, remembering Allah's command to stand for justice.

10. Patience:

Patience is essential in Islam. Prophet Ayyub's story of enduring illness is a model for believers (Surah Sad, 38:41-44).

Aminah faces difficulties at school but remembers Prophet Ayyub's patience, trusting in Allah's plan.

As parents and educators, our responsibility is to instill these Islamic values and morals in our children. Through nurturing respect, humility, responsibility, and other virtues, we prepare them to excel in this world and the Hereafter. By following the examples of the Prophets and righteous predecessors, we ensure their success in both worlds.

Yusuf, the fourth child in his family, grew up with three older sisters, each between four and eight years older than him. His birth was a long-awaited blessing, as his parents had fervently prayed for a son. His sisters, thrilled to have a younger brother to care for, lavished attention on him. Whenever Yusuf cried or gestured toward something he wanted, his family would immediately respond, fulfilling his needs without requiring him to articulate them verbally. Consequently, Yusuf's verbal development lagged, as his reliance on nonverbal communication was reinforced by his family's constant attention.

As Yusuf entered toddlerhood, he began noticing his sisters engaging in activities like swimming, riding bikes, and writing—activities that were beyond his abilities. His attempts to imitate his older siblings often resulted in frustration and tears. Whenever this occurred, his family would quickly offer comfort by providing him with treats or piggyback rides, inadvertently reinforcing his dependency on external comfort during moments of distress. This behavior pattern contributed to Yusuf's delayed speech development and hindered his ability to express himself verbally. His parents, overwhelmed with the demands of raising four children, frequently gave in to Yusuf's tantrums to maintain harmony within the household.

In a similar scenario, a mother named Fatima, from Saudi Arabia, noticed that her youngest child, Ahmed, was facing similar struggles. Ahmed, much like Yusuf, was frequently assisted by his older siblings whenever he cried or expressed frustration. Fatima, after listening to lectures by prominent scholars realized that this dynamic was inhibiting Ahmed's growth. She made a conscious decision to encourage Ahmed to take on tasks independently, giving him the space to experience frustration and ultimately overcome it. Though challenging at first, Ahmed gradually developed greater resilience and independence, embodying the principles of patience and perseverance that the companions of the Prophet (peace be upon him) were known for. This approach aligned with the teachings found in Tarbiyat al-Awlad fi al-Islam by Abdullah Nasih Ulwan, which emphasizes the importance of nurturing resilience and autonomy in children from a young age.

When Yusuf began kindergarten, he was excited by the prospect of riding the school bus like his older sisters. However, the structured environment of the classroom presented him with new challenges. Yusuf grew frustrated when his teachers and classmates had difficulty understanding him, and he became upset when expected to perform tasks on his own, such as opening his juice box or hanging up his coat. These experiences often led to emotional outbursts, highlighting Yusuf's lack of independence and emotional regulation skills.

A similar scenario occurred with a boy named Hasan, who also struggled with adjusting to school for the first time. His parents, after attending a lecture by an Islamic scholar following the ways of the Salaf, decided to adopt a more intentional approach to help Hasan manage his emotions and build independence. They began by gradually assigning him simple tasks, such as packing his own schoolbag and selecting his clothes for the day. Over time, Hasan grew more confident in his abilities, and his anxiety regarding school diminished. This approach encourages parents to nurture a child's ability to rely on their own strengths and patience during difficult times.

Emotional Intelligence and Independence

Yusuf's family could have taken steps to foster his emotional intelligence by encouraging him to communicate verbally rather than relying on gestures. For instance, when Yusuf pointed at a toy, his parents could have responded by acknowledging his feelings and encouraging him to express his desires verbally. This approach promotes the idea that guiding a child to articulate their feelings builds both emotional intelligence and self-awareness.

In the self-help book Raising an Emotionally Intelligent Child by John Gottman, it is emphasized that labeling emotions helps children better understand and manage their feelings. By helping children, like Yusuf, identify their emotions, parents can empower them to handle their frustrations more effectively. This method mirrors the teachings of the Prophet Muhammad (peace be upon him), who communicated with children in ways that helped them develop both intellectually and emotionally.

Similarly, encouraging Yusuf to perform simple tasks independently, such as dressing himself or opening his juice box, would have promoted his sense of autonomy. This aligns with the teachings advocates for gradually assigning children responsibilities to build their independence and character.

Stress Management

Yusuf's emotional outbursts in kindergarten indicate his difficulty managing stress. Shielding children from all forms of discomfort can prevent them from developing the necessary coping skills for life's challenges. In Tafsir al-Qurtubi, the commentary on Surah Al-Baqarah, 2:155, reminds us that tests and trials are part of Allah's plan to strengthen our character. Children, too, must be allowed to experience manageable challenges so they can learn resilience.

Abdullah, a father from Riyadh, took this approach when his two sons frequently argued over toys. Inspired by the teachings of the Quran and Hadith, Abdullah allowed his children to resolve their disputes on their own, stepping in only when necessary. This helped his sons develop better conflict resolution skills and manage stress more effectively, aligning with the wisdom of Tuhfat al-Mawdud by Ibn al-Qayyim which emphasizes the importance of patience in raising children.

Impulse Control

Another area where Yusuf struggled was impulse control, a common issue for young children. The Prophet Muhammad (peace be upon him) taught that true strength lies in controlling one's anger and impulses, as mentioned in a hadith reported in Sahih Muslim. Teaching children techniques such as deep breathing or counting can help them develop better self-control over time.

A modern example of this is found in The Marshmallow Test by Walter Mischel, which explores the long-term benefits of teaching children delayed gratification. In Islam, the emphasis on patience and self-control is foundational to building a strong character. Encouraging children to wait patiently and manage their emotions not only aligns with psychological best practices but also with Islamic teachings.

Yusuf's challenges with independence and emotional regulation highlight the importance of a balanced parenting approach that fosters both love and discipline. This style, grounded in Islamic teachings, reflects the example of the Prophet Muhammad (peace be upon him) and the righteous caliphs, who raised children to be emotionally intelligent, resilient, and rooted in their faith.

Eight-year-old Aisha had always loved the water. From the time she was a baby, she would joyfully splash in the bathtub. As a preschooler, she eagerly jumped into pools. By the time she was six, Aisha had joined her neighborhood swim team, and her swimming skills progressed quickly. By age eight, she was winning most of her races. Soon, her parents were approached by a female coach wearing Hijab and Niqaab from a year-round swim club who suggested signing her up for Muslim swim club where all Islamic principles were followed. Recognizing her talent, Aisha's parents thought joining the Muslim swim club would help her develop further. The coach only required three practices a week, and Aisha's parents believed the extra exercise would benefit her and help her sleep better, so they signed her up.

Aisha initially felt excited about joining the year-round swim team since swimming was something she loved, but she also cherished her time playing soccer with her friends, many of whom were in the same swim club. In fact, several of her friends from the soccer team were also part of the swimming team, balancing both sports without issue. Aisha admired their ability to do so and expressed her desire to continue playing soccer while swimming.

Her parents were initially hesitant, concerned that the time commitment might be too much for Aisha. However, they were also reminded of the Islamic teachings of moderation and balance. Allah instructs in the Quran, "Thus, We have made you a just community (a middle nation) that you will be witnesses over the people, and the Messenger will be a witness over you." (Quran 2:143). The Prophet Muhammad (peace be upon him) consistently practiced balance in his life and acts of worship, teaching the importance of avoiding extremes. This applies to parents as well, encouraging them to create a balanced schedule for their children, allowing them to pursue activities they love while not overburdening them.

Aisha's parents decided to support her in joining both the swim club and the soccer team, seeing that many of her friends managed to balance the two sports. They believed this would give her a well-rounded experience and help her maintain her excitement for both activities.

In "Child Education in Islam" by Abdullah Nasih Ulwan, he emphasizes the need for a balanced approach in raising children, one that includes discipline, religious education, and recreation. This reflects Aisha's situation where the balance between swimming and soccer, while surrounded by friends in both activities, contributes to a fulfilling and joyful childhood. The wisdom of Islamic scholars teaches us that balance is not only crucial in worship but also in daily life, including children's education and extracurricular activities.

Medical Insights:

Research in child development also supports the idea of maintaining a balance between activities. In "Developmental Psychology: Childhood and Adolescence" by David R. Shaffer and Katherine Kipp, they highlight that children who engage in diverse activities often show more well-rounded development. In Aisha's case, the combination of soccer and swimming gave her different types of exercise, socialization, and joy, which helped her avoid burnout in either activity.

Furthermore, according to "Child and Adolescent Psychiatry: A Comprehensive Textbook" edited by Melvin Lewis, maintaining a balance between structured activities and leisure time can protect children from experiencing mental health issues such as anxiety and stress. Aisha's decision to participate in both sports, with the support of her parents, allows her to enjoy her hobbies without being overwhelmed by the intensity of one single activity.

Allowing children the freedom to participate in multiple activities promotes better emotional and physical health. Doctors advise parents to let children explore their interests and to maintain balance in extracurricular commitments, emphasizing that diversity in activities can prevent emotional exhaustion.

Emotional and Psychological Considerations:

Aisha loved playing soccer with her friends, many of whom were also part of the swim team. Her weekends were filled with both activities, giving her a sense of fulfillment and excitement. On Saturday mornings, she would head to soccer practice and games, where she enjoyed the camaraderie and fast-paced environment. Then, in the afternoons, she would join her friends at swim practice. Her schedule was busy, but because she enjoyed both sports, she didn't feel pressured or overburdened.

In Islam, parental guidance should always consider the emotional and psychological well-being of the child. The Prophet (peace be upon him) said, "Allah loves kindness in everything" (Sahih Muslim). Aisha's parents demonstrated this kindness by allowing her to pursue both swimming and soccer, respecting her desires and fostering her emotional well-being. This reflects the importance of balance and empathy in raising children.

Additionally, "Kaplan and Sadock's Synopsis of Psychiatry" emphasizes the importance of fostering emotional resilience in children by giving them opportunities to engage in activities they enjoy. When children are allowed to explore their interests, they tend to develop better emotional health and greater resilience against stress and anxiety. Aisha's parents helped her achieve this balance, creating a nurturing environment where she could thrive both physically and emotionally.

Fostering Emotional Resilience:

The competitive nature of both swimming and soccer did sometimes lead to moments of anxiety for Aisha. Before her big swim meet in March, Aisha felt nervous, and on the morning of the competition, she experienced an upset stomach. Her performance wasn't as good as she had hoped, but her parents reassured her that what mattered most was her effort. They reminded her that she had both soccer and swimming as enjoyable activities, and that the outcome of a single race didn't define her success.

Doctors emphasize the importance of helping children understand that success is not always measured by winning but by effort and enjoyment. They note that performance anxiety in competitive settings is normal but can be mitigated when children feel supported and not pressured to meet unrealistic expectations. This approach is echoed in the teachings of the Prophet Muhammad (peace be upon him), who emphasized fostering independence and self-development in children. He said, "There is no gift that a father gives to his children better than good manners." (Sunan at-Tirmidhi). Aisha's parents exemplified this by encouraging her to enjoy both her sports without pressure.

As the swim season ended, Aisha's parents allowed her to continue playing soccer while maintaining her involvement in the swim team, ensuring that both activities brought her joy and fulfillment. They made sure that Aisha's schedule was balanced and that she had time for relaxation and family. This balance allowed her to continue excelling in both sports without feeling overwhelmed or burnt out.

Aisha's experience highlights how balance, emotional support, and parental understanding can help young children grow into emotionally resilient individuals who are strong in their faith and capable of navigating life's challenges.

Life frequently presents us with significant choices, such as deciding whether to stay home to care for your children or return to work, or whether to accept a promotion that could ease financial pressures and provide more fulfilling work but requires more time away from family. To navigate these important decisions in adulthood successfully, it is crucial to practice and learn from smaller decisions during childhood.

Consider the example of four-year-old Abdullah. Each morning, his mother carefully selected his clothes for daycare, thus removing his opportunity to make even simple choices about his attire. Imagine if Abdullah wanted to wear mismatched stripes and plaids or chose to wear shorts on a cold day. These small choices serve as valuable learning opportunities about the consequences of decisions. For instance, if Abdullah decides to wear shorts on a chilly day, he might feel uncomfortable. This experience teaches him the importance of choosing appropriate clothing based on the weather, providing him with a foundational lesson for making more complex decisions later in life.

Islamic teachings emphasize the importance of fostering independence and responsibility from a young age. The Prophet Muhammad (peace be upon him) encouraged allowing children to grow into capable and wise individuals. For example, he involved young companions like Abdullah ibn Abbas (may Allah be pleased with him) in decision-making processes. Abdullah ibn Abbas, known for his profound knowledge and wise counsel, benefited from such guidance in his formative years. The Prophet Muhammad (peace be upon him) entrusted young companions with responsibilities, reflecting the importance of nurturing independence and wisdom from an early age.

Abdullah also had no say in what foods he ate. Although his parents acted with good intentions, believing they knew what was best, they inadvertently removed his opportunities to practice decision-making. For instance, if Abdullah is restricted to only eating certain foods and never allowed to choose, he misses the chance to learn about balanced decisions. While it is essential to ensure that food choices are appropriate and healthy, providing Abdullah with options within permissible boundaries allows him to practice making responsible decisions.

The Prophet Muhammad (peace be upon him) demonstrated the importance of letting children experience the consequences of their actions. He used patience and understanding rather than harsh punishment. For example, he said, "The strong person is not the good wrestler; rather, the strong person is the one who controls himself when he is angry" (Sahih al-Bukhari). This hadith underscores the importance of self-control and wise decision-making, principles valuable in teaching children about natural and logical consequences.

Natural consequences occur without adult intervention. For example, if Abdullah insists on wearing shorts on a cold day and feels cold, that discomfort is a natural consequence of his choice. This experience helps him learn to consider weather conditions in the future. Similarly, logical consequences involve some parental input but are directly related to the child's decision. If Abdullah wants cookies and eats too many, he may become ill (a natural consequence), or his parents might decide not to buy cookies in the future (a logical consequence). Both scenarios help Abdullah understand the outcomes of his actions and enhance his decision-making skills.

The skill of reality testing—gathering information and interpreting it accurately to support sound decision-making—aligns with Islamic principles of accountability. As the Prophet Muhammad (peace be upon him) emphasized, "The intelligent person is the one who controls himself and is patient in adversity" (Sahih al-Bukhari). This reflects the importance of self-discipline and making wise choices, which aids children like Abdullah in analyzing situations and making informed decisions.

Medical and psychological literature supports the importance of decision-making practice from an early age. For instance, "Developmental-Behavioral Pediatrics" by William B. Carey highlights that the development of executive functions, including decision-making, is crucial for adaptive behavior. Similarly, "Handbook of Child Psychology" by Richard M. Lerner emphasizes how early experiences shape cognitive and emotional skills. Medscape articles, such as "The Impact of Early Childhood Decisions on Adolescent Development," underline that early decision-making experiences foster problem-solving skills and emotional intelligence.

In psychiatry, Dr. Dan Siegel's "The Whole-Brain Child" underscores the significance of teaching children to make decisions and understand their consequences. He emphasizes that children who experience natural and logical consequences develop better self-regulation and problem-solving skills. This aligns with advice from Dr. William Stixrud, who in his lectures on cognitive development, advocates for allowing children to face the outcomes of their choices to build resilience and independence.

Books from Darussalam and other Islamic salaf publishers also emphasize the importance of teaching children to make responsible decisions within the framework of Islamic values. These sources reflect how providing children with opportunities to make choices, while guiding them with wisdom, supports their development into responsible and capable individuals.

Ultimately, allowing children to experience the consequences of their decisions within safe boundaries teaches them valuable lessons. Experience becomes a great teacher, helping children grow in wisdom, independence, and emotional intelligence. This preparation is crucial not only for fulfilling their responsibilities in this life but also for their preparation for the hereafter.

It is disheartening to see children struggle with changes, become overly anxious, or give up easily. The ability to persist and maintain an optimistic outlook can help children overcome many obstacles, leading to healthier self-regard and emotional well-being.

Consider the case of Aisha. As the eldest of six children, Aisha had two younger sisters and three younger brothers. Her family had established a comfortable routine in their life. Aisha's father, for example, always started his day early, waking Aisha and her siblings to kiss them goodbye before heading to the gym and then to work. Her mother prepared a hot breakfast for the children and took them to school. After school, they would return home, prepare a snack together, and then complete homework. The routine continued with an hour of outdoor play or reading and then enjoying Islamic lectures while her mother made dinner. The family would have dinner together at 6 P.M., followed by bath time, bedtime reading, and lights out by 8 P.M.

Due to a change in family circumstances, Aisha's mother had to start working full-time when Aisha was eight. As a trained nurse, Aisha's mother took a 7 A.M. to 7 P.M. shift at the local hospital on Mondays,

Tuesdays, and Wednesdays. This change significantly altered their routine. Aisha was awakened by her father, who instead of preparing a hot breakfast, gave her and her siblings cereal. He dropped them off at a neighbor's house to wait for the school bus. After school, they had to ride the bus home and were then cared for by an elderly female aunty until their father returned from work around six. Dinner times shifted, with Aisha and her siblings trying to wait until 7:30 P.M. to eat with their mother. However, they became very hungry and whiny by then, which affected their bath and bedtime routine.

Although their parents explained the changes to the children, they framed the situation negatively by expressing sentiments such as, "We wish mommy didn't have to go back to work" and "This is going to be really hard for all of us." They also mentioned, "Riding the bus probably won't be as fun as having mommy take you, but lots of kids do it." While their intentions were honest, this negative framing made it harder for Aisha and her siblings to adjust. It would have been more beneficial to present the changes in a neutral or positive manner.

In a case similar to Aisha's, consider the example of Fatima, whose family faced a significant change when her father lost his job. Fatima's parents chose to remain positive and focused on the new opportunities this change could bring. They explained to Fatima that her father was exploring new career paths and that they might have to adjust their spending, but it was a temporary situation. They involved her in setting new family routines and highlighted the positive aspects, such as spending more time together at home. This approach helped Fatima remain resilient and optimistic during the transition.

In the self-help book The 7 Habits of Highly Effective People by Stephen R. Covey, Covey discusses the importance of a positive mindset and proactive approach to change. He emphasizes that viewing challenges as opportunities rather than obstacles can greatly enhance one's ability to adapt and thrive. This principle aligns with how Aisha's parents could have approached the situation—by framing the changes as opportunities for new experiences and growth.

Similarly, in Mindset: The New Psychology of Success by Carol S. Dweck, Dweck explores how a growth mindset can significantly impact children's ability to handle challenges. Children who are taught to view setbacks as part of the learning process are more likely to develop resilience and adaptability. This concept reflects how Aisha could have benefited from a more positive framing of the changes.

From a medical perspective, the textbook Developmental-Behavioral Pediatrics highlights how children's reactions to change can be managed effectively with appropriate support and communication. It emphasizes that children who receive reassurance and positive reinforcement during transitions are more likely to develop adaptive coping strategies. This supports the idea that Aisha's parents could have benefitted from framing the changes in a more supportive and encouraging manner.

Psychiatry textbooks, such as Child and Adolescent Psychiatry by David W. Brown, discuss the role of parental attitudes in shaping children's responses to stress and change. Positive reinforcement and constructive communication are key strategies in helping children adapt, reflecting the need for Aisha's parents to adopt a more positive and encouraging approach.

Medscape articles on childhood anxiety suggest that children exposed to negative framing during significant changes may experience increased anxiety and resistance. They recommend proactive strategies such as involving children in the process and maintaining an optimistic outlook to mitigate these effects. This insight aligns with the need for Aisha's parents to reframe their communication to foster better adjustment.

Child psychologists emphasizes the importance of maintaining a positive environment during family transitions. They advocate for explaining changes in a manner that highlights potential benefits and supports, which can significantly ease children's adjustment. This advice underscores the importance of how Aisha's parents communicated the changes to her.

The importance of positive parental influence and maintaining a supportive environment is emphasized. Parents can foster resilience in their children through constructive communication and supportive behavior.

In the Quran, Allah says, "Indeed, with hardship comes ease" (Quran 94:6). This verse encourages believers to maintain patience and optimism during difficult times, showing that challenges are accompanied by relief. The Prophet Muhammad (peace be upon him) also taught the importance of patience and optimism through his own life. For example, during the Battle of Uhud, he encouraged his companions to persevere and remain hopeful, demonstrating that overcoming difficulties leads to greater rewards.

Additionally, during the time of the Caliphs, the leadership of Umar ibn al-Khattab (may Allah be pleased with him) is noted for its emphasis on patience and perseverance. He said, "Sometimes the people who are closest to us become the most distant, and the people who are the most distant become the closest." This wisdom reflects the importance of adapting to changes with a positive mindset and finding strength in difficult situations.

Furthermore, the Prophet Muhammad (peace be upon him) advised in a Hadith: "The strong person is not the one who overcomes others; rather, the strong person is the one who controls himself when he is angry" (Sahih al-Bukhari). This Hadith emphasizes self-control and resilience, principles that can be applied when guiding children through changes.

In addition to the inability to adjust to change (a lack of flexibility), Aisha and her siblings also faced increased stress, which impacted their sleep and interactions with their parents. Flexibility and optimism are key for managing stress. Children who lack these skills may struggle with additional challenges.

The case studies highlight that loving and involved parents may still need to focus on fostering emotional intelligence in their children. It is crucial to examine how parental modeling, parenting styles, and discipline strategies contribute to developing a child's emotional intelligence.

By aligning with these approaches and maintaining an Islamic perspective, parents can better prepare their children to handle life's changes with resilience and positive thinking, reflecting the values taught by the Prophet Muhammad (peace be upon him) and the wisdom found in the Quran and Hadith.

Chapter 3

Imagine Aisha, a fifth-grader, standing nervously at the front of her school companions, preparing to give her first speech. As she looks at her notes and then at her classmates, time seems to stretch endlessly. Her heart races, and her anxiety surges.

Aisha feels overwhelmed and wishes she could escape. She glances at her teacher, who offers a reassuring nod. As Aisha starts her speech, she stumbles over her words and mispronounces a few terms. Her classmates begin to giggle, making her feel as though the entire world is mocking her. Even her teacher struggles to suppress a smile before asking the class to be quiet.

Feeling paralyzed and humiliated, Aisha wishes she could run home but instead hurries through her speech as quietly as possible, her fear of further ridicule evident.

This scenario reflects common childhood experiences where we feel embarrassed and alone.

From a psychological perspective, Aisha's reaction can be understood through the lens of stress response mechanisms. When Aisha stood before her class, her heart raced, her face flushed, and her hands became clammy due to her body's stress response: the amygdala detected a threat and triggered the release of hormones like adrenaline and cortisol, putting her body on high alert. According to Principles and Practice of Stress Management by Paul M. Lehrer, this response is an evolutionary mechanism designed to help us manage immediate threats.

The stress response caused Aisha's senses to sharpen but impaired her higher cognitive functions, leading to difficulties in problem-solving and focus. Her body's "fight or flight" reaction, as described by Dr. Peter Levine in Waking the Tiger: Healing Trauma, escalated into a "freeze response," similar to how opossums play dead to avoid predators. This led to trembling hands and an uneasy stomach, with her brain forming neural pathways that associated public speaking with danger. Repeated exposure to negative experiences reinforces these pathways, making the distressing memory vivid and impactful. Dr. Bessel van der Kolk's The Body Keeps the Score discusses how such traumatic experiences can lead to long-term psychological effects.

Research underscores the significant impact of stress on children's well-being. The American Psychological Association notes that nearly one-third of children experience physical symptoms of stress, such as headaches and stomachaches. A Medscape report highlights that childhood stress is linked to various health issues, including anxiety and depression, emphasizing the importance of early intervention.

Two years later, as a seventh-grader, Aisha faces a new challenge: her teacher announces that each student must give a speech on their favorite book. Despite her love for reading, the prospect of speaking in front of the class triggers intense anxiety. She seeks an alternative from her teacher, who reassures her not to worry.

Aisha's ongoing panic affects her sleep and social interactions. On speech day, she speaks slowly and quietly but still makes mistakes, leading to more laughter from her classmates. Receiving a C on her speech reinforces her belief that she is incapable of public speaking and leads her to avoid similar situations. The Anxiety and Phobia Workbook by Edmund J. Bourne explains how avoidance can temporarily alleviate anxiety but often exacerbates the problem in the long run, limiting personal and professional growth.

This scenario mirrors the experiences of early Muslims who faced mockery and persecution for their beliefs. The Prophet Muhammad (peace be upon him) and his companions endured harsh treatment by the Quraysh tribe, demonstrating the importance of steadfastness and composure in the face of adversity.

At 32, despite her hard work and experience, Aisha's fear of public speaking continues to hinder her career advancement, manifesting as physical symptoms like shaking hands and a churning stomach during presentations. This is similar to insights from Dr. Susan Jeffers' Feel the Fear and Do It Anyway, which discusses how avoidance can limit personal and professional growth and emphasizes the importance of confronting fears to build resilience.

Had Aisha been provided with tools to manage her stress and fear from the beginning, her experience might have been different. Supportive feedback grounded in patience and resilience, akin to the teachings of the Prophet Muhammad (peace be upon him), could have fostered her confidence and personal growth. The Prophet Muhammad (peace be upon him) exemplified patience and positive reinforcement. He said, "The strong person is not the one who overcomes others; rather, the strong person is the one who controls himself when he is angry" (Sahih al-Bukhari). This Hadith emphasizes managing emotions and staying resilient.

The Quran also provides guidance on handling difficulties with patience and optimism: "Indeed, with hardship comes ease" (Quran 94:6). This verse reflects the promise of relief following challenges and encourages believers to remain hopeful and steadfast.

Dr. Daniel Levitin's research in The Organized Mind highlights the importance of emotional support in overcoming stress. The Prophet Muhammad (peace be upon him) demonstrated empathy and support during the Ta'if incident, where he faced hostility and rejection but remained patient and persevered.

If Aisha's situation had been approached with a supportive and constructive perspective, aligned with Islamic principles, it could have fostered her resilience and growth. Providing Aisha with a supportive environment could have helped her overcome her fears and develop confidence, reflecting the teachings of Islam on emotional well-being and personal growth.

Aisha's Mother Feels Guilty

In the context of Aisha's story, Aisha's mother might experience feelings of guilt over her daughter's struggles with public speaking. This guilt could stem from various sources, such as feeling responsible for Aisha's early negative experience, believing she failed to provide adequate support, or feeling that she could have intervened earlier.

To address this, it's important to consider the following points:

1. Understanding Guilt and Responsibility:

Guilt often arises when we believe we have not met our own standards or expectations. However, in Islam, we are encouraged to acknowledge our mistakes and seek forgiveness from Allah while also striving to rectify them. In the Quran, Allah says: "And those who, when they commit an immorality or wrong themselves by their own souls, remember Allah and ask forgiveness for their sins" (Surah Al-Imran, 3:135). This verse highlights the importance of turning to Allah for forgiveness and seeking ways to improve our actions.

2. Role of Parents:

Parents play a crucial role in supporting and guiding their children, but they are not infallible. The Prophet Muhammad (peace be upon him) advised parents to be patient and compassionate with their children. In an authentic Hadith, he said: "The best of you are those who are the best to their families" (Sunan Ibn Majah). This Hadith underscores the importance of kindness and understanding in parenting, rather than focusing on guilt.

3. Proactive Steps:

Instead of dwelling on guilt, Aisha's mother can take proactive steps to support her daughter. Encouraging Aisha to use techniques like mindfulness in Salah (prayer), which can help manage stress and overcome fears, is one way to provide positive support. Additionally, reinforcing Aisha's strengths and achievements can help build her confidence.

4. Islamic Teachings on Forgiveness and Self-Improvement:

Islam encourages self-improvement and personal growth.

5. Seeking Professional Guidance:

If feelings of guilt are overwhelming, Aisha's mother might benefit from seeking guidance from a counselor or therapist who understands Islamic perspectives. This can help her address her feelings constructively and support her daughter more effectively.

6. Integration of Islamic Teachings:

Integrating Islamic teachings into daily life can offer comfort and guidance. The Quran states: "Indeed, with hardship comes ease" (Surah Ash-Sharh, 94:6). This verse reminds us that challenges are accompanied by opportunities for growth and relief.

By focusing on positive actions, seeking forgiveness, and using Islamic teachings as a guide, Aisha's mother can address her feelings of guilt and support her daughter in overcoming her challenges.

Types of Parental Guilt

In parenting, there are three main types of guilt that one may experience:

Appropriate guilt serves as a valuable indicator that your actions may be misaligned with your values, prompting positive changes. For instance, consider a mother named Aisha who feels remorse after raising her voice at her daughter, Fatima. This guilt can lead Aisha to reflect on her behavior and explore more constructive approaches to discipline. The Prophet Muhammad (peace be upon him) emphasized the importance of kindness and patience in parenting, stating, "The best of you are those who are best to their families" (Sunan Ibn Majah). This type of guilt can motivate Aisha to manage her stress better and adopt a more empathetic approach to parenting.

Dr. Brené Brown, in her book "The Gifts of Imperfection," highlights how acknowledging and addressing our imperfections with self-compassion can lead to personal growth and improved relationships. This principle is evident in Aisha's experience, where her guilt becomes an opportunity for self-improvement and better parenting.

According to "Principles and Practice of Pediatric Sleep Medicine" by Richard Ferber, emotional responses like guilt can affect parenting practices and a child's emotional well-being. Understanding and addressing appropriate guilt can contribute to more effective and supportive parenting.

Appropriate guilt is viewed as a chance to realign one's parenting with Islamic values. Such guilt should be used constructively to improve parenting practices in light of the teachings of Islam.

In Aesop's fable "The Dog and His Reflection," the dog loses his reflection when he tries to grab it, showing that sometimes our desires and actions can lead us away from what truly matters. This can be paralleled with how appropriate guilt can help redirect actions towards better alignment with our values.

Unnecessary guilt often arises over trivial matters that do not significantly affect your child's well-being. For instance, Ahmed may feel guilty for not spending enough time outdoors with his children, Omar and Layla, due to his busy schedule. He worries about minor issues like bug bites from brief outdoor play. The Prophet Muhammad (peace be upon him) advised not to overburden oneself with excessive concerns, stating, "The strong person is not the one who is good at wrestling. Rather, the strong person is the one who controls himself when he is angry" (Sahih al-Bukhari). Ahmed's guilt about minor issues should not overshadow the positive aspects of his parenting.

Dr. Carol Dweck's research in "Mindset: The New Psychology of Success" explores how perfectionism and unnecessary guilt can undermine self-acceptance. Ahmed's feelings highlight the importance of focusing on overall well-being rather than minor issues.

In "The Science of Parenting," Margot Sunderland addresses how undue guilt can lead to parental stress and affect a child's development. Recognizing and managing unnecessary guilt is crucial for maintaining healthy parenting practices.

In "The Islamic Perspective on Raising Children" by Dr. Muhammad Ali Alkhuli, the author discusses how unnecessary guilt often stems from unrealistic expectations. He emphasizes that parents should focus on the broader picture of their children's well-being rather than being overly concerned with minor details.

"Don't sweat the small stuff" is a proverb that captures the essence of not letting trivial matters cause undue stress or guilt. This aligns with the idea that unnecessary guilt over minor issues should be managed to focus on more significant aspects of parenting.

Chronic guilt involves persistent feelings of guilt without a clear reason. For instance, Fatima might constantly worry that she is failing to prepare her son, Yusuf, adequately for his future. This ongoing guilt can lead to unrealistic fears about her parenting decisions. The Caliph Umar ibn al-Khattab (may Allah be pleased with him) was known for his deep concern for justice and welfare but also demonstrated reliance on Allah without letting guilt overwhelm him. As reflected in the Quran: "And whoever relies upon Allah – then He is sufficient for him" (Quran 65:3). Fatima can find solace in seeking Allah's guidance and trusting in His plan.

Islamic figures such as Umar ibn al-Khattab exemplified how to manage guilt through faith and trust in Allah. This historical perspective helps parents like Fatima maintain perspective and manage chronic guilt effectively.

"Cognitive Behavioral Therapy for Anxiety and Depression" by David M. Clark and Christine A. Purdon explores how chronic guilt can be managed through cognitive restructuring. Addressing chronic guilt can prevent it from negatively impacting parenting.

An article on Medscape discusses how chronic guilt can contribute to burnout and mental health issues in parents. Strategies for managing chronic guilt, such as seeking support and focusing on self-care, can help mitigate its effects.

In "Islamic Parenting: Guidelines for Raising Children in Islam" by Dr. Muhammad al-Jibaly, chronic guilt is addressed from an Islamic perspective, emphasizing the importance of trust in Allah and seeking His guidance to overcome feelings of inadequacy.

"A stitch in time saves nine" highlights the importance of addressing issues promptly rather than letting them fester, which can be related to managing chronic guilt by taking proactive steps to address underlying concerns.

Many parents, particularly working mothers, experience significant guilt. For instance, Aisha, a working mother, might feel torn between her professional responsibilities and her desire to be a perfect parent. Despite her efforts, she may feel inadequate compared to the idealized image of stay-at-home mothers. The Quran advises balance and moderation: "And do not waste [resources], for indeed, He does not like the wasteful" (Quran 7:31).

Stephen Covey's "The 7 Habits of Highly Effective People" advocates for balancing personal and professional life to maintain overall well-being. Aisha's struggle reflects the importance of focusing on meaningful interactions rather than comparing oneself to idealized standards.

In "Burnout in Families," Dr. William J. Doherty examines how working parents can manage feelings of inadequacy and guilt by setting realistic expectations and seeking support. Recognizing the need for balance can help alleviate excessive guilt.

The tale of the "Tortoise and the Hare" illustrates the value of steady, consistent efforts over comparing oneself to others. The tortoise's persistence in the race, despite the hare's quick start, demonstrates the importance of focusing on one's path rather than comparing oneself to others.

Parents often compare their parenting to others', influenced by social media and societal expectations. For example, Ahmed might feel inadequate when he sees other parents posting about their children's achievements online. This comparison can lead to feelings of inadequacy and the belief that he is not doing enough. Focusing on personal growth and internal righteousness is more valuable than external comparisons. Ahmed's comparison to idealized portrayals of parenting can hinder self-acceptance and personal growth.

An article on Medscape discusses how social media comparisons can contribute to parental stress and decreased self-esteem. Understanding and managing these comparisons can help maintain a healthier perspective on parenting.

"Comparison is the thief of joy" is a proverb that underscores the negative impact of comparing oneself to others, emphasizing the importance of appreciating one's own efforts and progress.

Parenting out of guilt can lead to unhealthy practices. For instance, Aisha might excessively indulge her child's requests to alleviate her guilt, which can result in inconsistent parenting and undermine her child's sense of security. The Prophet Muhammad (peace be upon him) emphasized balanced and just parenting, saying, "Fear Allah and be just among your children" (Sahih al-Bukhari). Parenting should be guided by fairness and consistency rather than guilt.

Dr. Daniel J. Siegel and Dr. Tina Payne Bryson's "The Whole-Brain Child" advocates for balanced and consistent parenting strategies that support healthy child development. Aisha's approach should focus on maintaining a stable and nurturing environment rather than reacting to guilt.

In "Parenting with PTSD," Dr. Carla Marie Manly explores how excessive guilt can lead to inconsistent parenting practices. Strategies for managing guilt and maintaining consistency can support positive child development.

In the fable "The Fox and the Grapes," the fox, unable to reach the grapes, dismisses them as sour. This can be related to how guilt-driven decisions may lead to justifying actions that are not in the child's best interest. Maintaining consistency and fairness, rather than reacting to guilt, is crucial.

Excessive guilt can lead to various behaviors:

- A parent might avoid personal activities or downtime to prevent feelings of guilt about taking a break. For instance, Fatima might skip her relaxation time to ensure she is constantly available for her children.

- A parent may give in to a child's demands temporarily to feel better about themselves, even if it's not beneficial for the child. For example, Ahmed might buy extra toys for his children to compensate for not spending enough time with them.

- Allowing special privileges or leniencies to ease one's guilty conscience, which doesn't address underlying issues. For example, Aisha might permit her children to stay up late to make up for not spending enough time with them during the day.

Responding to guilt trips from children or others can encourage emotional manipulation. For instance, if a parent consistently gives in to a child's pleas out of guilt, it may set a precedent for emotional manipulation. Consistency and firmness in decision-making are essential for maintaining authority and ensuring respect for boundaries. The Prophet Muhammad (peace be upon him) exemplified steadfastness and justice, advising against giving in to manipulation that goes against what is right.

Dr. John Gottman's "The 7 Principles for Making Marriage Work" emphasizes the importance of setting clear boundaries and not allowing guilt to dictate parenting decisions. Consistent and fair parenting prevents children from using guilt to manipulate situations.

An article on Medscape highlights the potential for emotional manipulation in family dynamics and suggests strategies for maintaining authority while addressing emotional needs. Balancing firmness with empathy can help prevent manipulative behavior.

"Give an inch, and they'll take a mile" underscores the risk of setting a precedent for manipulation if boundaries are not maintained. Consistent and fair parenting helps in setting and respecting boundaries effectively.

Managing parental guilt involves understanding its various forms and impacts, focusing on the quality of time spent with children, and avoiding responses driven solely by guilt. Aligning parenting practices with Islamic values, seeking forgiveness from Allah, and striving for self-improvement can help parents navigate these challenges more effectively, guided by the Quran and the teachings of the Prophet Muhammad (peace be upon him).

Many parents, like Umm Salamah, might experience guilt with thoughts such as "I don't spend enough time with them." They may struggle to determine whether the solution lies in changing their behavior or managing their emotions.

To address these feelings of guilt, it is crucial first to understand the reasons behind them and observe their impact on your actions. This self-awareness will guide you in determining the appropriate course of action.

To determine whether your guilt is justified, consider these four questions:

1. Did I do something that negatively affected my child?

For example, if you have been allowing your child to spend even a minute watching TV, or if you reacted harshly and said something hurtful, it is important to correct your behavior. The Prophet Muhammad (peace be upon him) emphasized moderation in all aspects of life, including parenting, as reflected in his advice on balance and discipline (Sahih Muslim).

Ahmed, a father, noticed his teenage daughter Aisha was present on social media. This he realized had led to decreased focus on her studies. Ahmed therefore asked his daughter to delete all her social media accounts and became more involved in Aisha's academic life.

The American Academy of Pediatrics recommends that parents set consistent limits on screen time and engage in interactive activities with their children to promote better developmental outcomes.

In "The Fox and the Grapes," the fox, who is unable to reach the grapes, dismisses them as sour. This fable teaches that sometimes we rationalize our failures or shortcomings instead of addressing them directly. Like the fox, parents might justify leniency in screen time without taking action to correct it.

2. Is there something I can change?

If your guilt relates to a past event, such as a divorce from three years ago, you cannot change the past. However, if you feel guilty about not encouraging your child to complete their homework, you can take steps to be more supportive and involved moving forward.

Fatimah felt remorseful for not being more involved in her son Bilal's education after a recent move. She addressed this by creating a study schedule and dedicating time each day to assist Bilal with his homework. This proactive approach allowed her to make meaningful changes in her parenting.

The Rights of Children in Islam by Dr. Muhammad Ali Al-Hashimi emphasizes the importance of continuous self-improvement and making amends for past shortcomings. Al-Hashimi advocates for focusing on present actions to improve one's situation, in line with the teachings of the Prophet Muhammad (peace be upon him).

The concept of cognitive restructuring, discussed in Feeling Good: The New Mood Therapy by David D. Burns, involves shifting focus from past mistakes to current actionable steps to improve one's situation and emotional well-being.

In the story of "The Tortoise and the Hare," the hare, who once boasted and lost to the slow but steady tortoise, learned that consistent effort outweighs past failures. Similarly, making adjustments in the present can correct past lapses.

3. What can I do differently?

Identify a specific, actionable step to enhance your parenting. For instance, instead of using your phone while spending time with your child, give them your full attention. Implementing a no-electronics rule in the house can reflect the Hadith emphasizing the significance of family time and undivided attention.

Layla realized she was often distracted by her phone during family dinners. She decided to leave her phone in another room during mealtimes to focus entirely on her children. This change improved family interactions and modeled mindfulness for her kids.

The Power of Now by Eckhart Tolle highlights the benefits of being fully present in interactions. Present-moment awareness during family time fosters deeper connections and emotional well-being.

Research published in JAMA Pediatrics indicates that parents' mindfulness practices can improve their interactions with children and enhance overall family dynamics (JAMA Pediatrics, 2023).

"The best way to predict the future is to create it." This proverb emphasizes taking proactive steps in the present to shape a positive future, reflecting the importance of focusing on current actions.

4. Is there something I should do to make amends with my child?

Apologizing to your child is not always necessary for minor mistakes, but it is appropriate for more significant issues. For instance, if you raised your voice in anger, it is important to acknowledge this by saying, "I am sorry for raising my voice. I was angry and should have managed my emotions better." This approach aligns with the Prophet's teachings on seeking forgiveness and maintaining good relationships (Sahih Bukhari).

Musa, who raised his voice during a heated moment, later apologized to his son Youssef, acknowledging his mistake and promising to manage his anger better. This act of making amends reinforced the importance of seeking forgiveness and improving relationships.

Maintaining good relationships and making amends is a significant part of personal development and following the teachings of the Prophet Muhammad (peace be upon him).

Dr. Dan Siegel's The Mindsight discusses the importance of acknowledging and addressing emotional mistakes to build healthier relationships and emotional resilience.

In the story of "The Prodigal Son," the father's forgiveness and acceptance of his son highlight the importance of making amends and the positive impact of forgiveness on relationships.

Feeling bad does not necessarily mean wrongdoing. Many parents fear that minor mistakes will have severe consequences for their child's future.

For example, a mother named Khadijah forgot to enroll her son, Ibrahim, in a summer camp. She feared this oversight would prevent Ibrahim from making friends and harm his future opportunities. Such predictions are often exaggerated. Missing one camp session is unlikely to have a lasting negative impact. The real issue may be the stress parents impose on themselves, which can affect the overall family environment.

Aisha, a mother, became overly concerned when she missed a parent-teacher meeting, fearing it would negatively impact her child's academic performance. However, the teacher assured her that one missed meeting would not affect her child's progress. This example illustrates how excessive worry can be more damaging than the actual issue.

"Don't cross the bridge until you come to it." This saying advises against worrying excessively about potential future problems that may never occur.

We often link specific parental actions to a child's behavior without sufficient evidence. Sometimes, assumptions are made without factual support.

A mother named Zaynab believed her child's learning difficulties were due to her occasional coffee consumption during pregnancy. Another mother thought that the non-organic vegetables might explain her child's health issues. Research indicates such fears are often unfounded.

Research in Principles of Psychotherapy by Rollo May emphasizes the importance of distinguishing between actual evidence and irrational fears in understanding child behavior and parental guilt.

In "The Goose that Laid the Golden Eggs," the farmer, driven by greed, kills the goose to get all the gold at once, only to find there were no more eggs. This fable illustrates the danger of drawing hasty conclusions and making decisions based on incorrect assumptions.

Forgiving yourself for mistakes is crucial. For instance, Zainab, who accidentally caused boiling soup to fall on her son Isa, felt intense guilt and believed she did not deserve happiness. Over time, she recognized the accident as an unfortunate event, not a reflection of her worth as a parent. Instead of self-criticism, she focused on supporting Isa and preventing similar incidents.

Sarah missed an important family event due to work commitments and felt profound guilt. She realized that constantly punishing herself was counterproductive. Instead, she focused on balancing her work and family life more effectively, aligning with the Islamic principle of self-compassion (Surah Az-Zumar 39:53).

"To err is human; to forgive, divine." This proverb underscores the importance of forgiveness, both towards oneself and others.

The notion that "good enough is never good enough" is prevalent, but research by D. W. Winnicott suggests that being a "good enough" parent is beneficial. Winnicott's studies showed that children of parents who are dedicated but imperfect grow up to be healthy and resilient.

Umm Ayman, a devoted mother, accepted her imperfections as part of her parenting journey. She focused on offering genuine love and effort, understanding that these qualities were more important than striving for unattainable perfection. Her children grew up to appreciate her dedication and balanced approach.

In "The Ant and the Grasshopper," the industrious ant is prepared for winter, while the carefree grasshopper is not. This fable demonstrates the value of consistent effort and balance, rather than striving for perfection, to achieve stability and resilience.

By integrating these insights from both Islamic teachings and contemporary psychological research, you can better navigate parental guilt, focusing on actionable steps, self-forgiveness, and balanced parenting.

Teaching Preschoolers Basic Concepts About Guilt

Research indicates that even young children begin to exhibit signs of guilt as early as two years old. For instance, a toddler like Ahmed might avoid eye contact after engaging in inappropriate behavior. At this stage, though they may not fully grasp the concept of guilt, it is an opportune time to introduce them to it within an Islamic framework.

In Islam, guilt is deeply connected to the concept of taubah (repentance), which entails feeling sincere remorse for one's sins and seeking forgiveness from Allah. The Prophet Muhammad (peace be upon him) emphasized this by saying, "Remorse is repentance." (Sunan Ibn Majah). For example, if your son Ahmed hurts his sibling or a friend, you should first comfort the victim. Say, "Oh no, I'm sorry you were hurt by what Ahmed did. Are you okay?" This reflects the mercy that the Prophet (peace be upon him) taught, much like how he comforted those who had been wronged.

This nurturing approach can be likened to the story of the Lion and the Mouse from Aesop's Fables, where the lion, despite being the more powerful animal, showed mercy to the mouse who later helped him in return. Similarly, teaching children mercy helps them understand the importance of repentance and rectification.

After ensuring the victim's well-being, instill a sense of responsibility in your child, aligning with Islamic teachings. The Prophet (peace be upon him) taught, "Help your brother, whether he is the oppressor or the oppressed." (Sahih Bukhari). In this context, you can discipline Ahmed by placing him in time-out or revoking a privilege, while making sure he understands that such behavior is unacceptable.

Alternatively, Ahmed could give his favorite toy to the person he hurt, reflecting the Islamic concept of compensation for harm.

For instance, consider a scenario where your son, Hamza, takes his sister's toy, causing her to cry. After comforting her, ask Hamza to give her his favorite book or toy for the day. This action fosters empathy, reflecting how Abu Bakr as-Siddiq (may Allah be pleased with him) would immediately seek to rectify any wrong he committed, showing his deep sense of remorse and responsibility.

This concept of making amends resonates with the well-known proverb, "An apology without change is just manipulation." Teaching children to follow through with sincere actions demonstrates that true repentance leads to positive change.

From a psychological perspective, studies show that children as young as toddlers can begin to experience basic forms of guilt, although their understanding is limited. According to child psychiatry textbooks, this is often expressed through avoidance behaviors, such as not making eye contact or distancing themselves from the scene. Pediatricians and child psychologists often recommend early intervention when it comes to teaching emotions like guilt. The goal is to help children process their actions in a healthy and emotionally productive way rather than suppress or internalize them.

Incorporating medical research from Medscape, experts advise that during this stage, parents should model emotional regulation and appropriate responses to mistakes, helping children understand that guilt should guide them to rectify their actions rather than immobilize them with shame. Creating a secure emotional environment where a child feels safe admitting their mistakes allows for better emotional and social development.

Fostering a sense of guilt in an Islamic way helps establish moral boundaries. Parents should start with mild reprimands and then follow up with encouragement for children to rectify their wrongs. This approach helps children internalize guilt positively, guiding them to repentance rather than fear of punishment.

Teaching School-Age Kids How to Deal with Guilt

Children aged five to eight often try to evade responsibility, which presents an opportunity to emphasize personal accountability and repentance according to Islamic teachings. For example, when your daughter Fatima lies to a friend or breaks her brother's toy, guide her towards restitution. You might ask, "You lied to your friend. How can you make it right?" or "You broke your brother's toy. What can you do to fix this?" These questions align with the Quranic teaching, "The recompense for an injury is an injury equal thereto (in degree); but if a person forgives and makes reconciliation, his reward is due from Allah." (Surah Ash-Shura, 42:40).

A real-life scenario could involve asking Fatima to apologize sincerely to her friend or offer to repair or replace her brother's toy. This mirrors the actions of Abu Bakr as-Siddiq (may Allah be pleased with him), who consistently sought to make amends whenever he wronged someone, demonstrating genuine remorse and accountability.

This lesson can be further reinforced with the famous story of The Boy Who Cried Wolf, where the boy's dishonesty led to dire consequences. It emphasizes how making amends and being truthful can build trust and maintain relationships.

Studies in developmental psychology note that children in this age group begin to understand the concept of fairness and justice, making it an ideal time to teach restitution and amends. Medical research further suggests that providing a structured opportunity for a child to correct their wrongdoings leads to healthier emotional development and a stronger sense of personal responsibility.

Medical textbooks also emphasize the importance of balance in guiding children to handle guilt appropriately. Pediatric neurologist Dr. Martha Farah, in a lecture on emotional development in children, mentioned that excessive or unresolved guilt can manifest in anxiety or behavioral issues later on. Therefore, helping a child like Fatima learn to resolve guilt by making amends not only aligns with Islamic teachings but also fosters healthier mental and emotional development.

Encouraging children to take responsibility for their actions, while maintaining a loving and supportive environment, ensures they don't develop unhealthy feelings of self-blame. The balance between gentle correction and guiding children towards repentance is considered key in Islamic pedagogy.

Teaching Teens That Guilt Trips Don't Work

By the time children reach their teenage years, they have a strong understanding of guilt and may use it to manipulate situations. For instance, a teen might say, "But all my friends' parents let them do it!" or "You never let me have any fun!" Responding calmly with acknowledgment of their feelings while maintaining firm Islamic values is key. For example, you could say, "I love you, and it is my duty as a parent to keep you safe." This reflects the Islamic principle of guiding children toward righteousness, as stated in the Quran: "O you who have believed, fear Allah and speak words of appropriate justice." (Surah Al-Ahzab, 33:70).

Research from Medscape and adolescent psychology textbooks emphasizes that guilt trips are detrimental to healthy parent-teen relationships, causing resentment and emotional distance. Experts on parenting teens, caution against using guilt to control behavior, recommending instead to focus on dialogue and reinforcing Islamic values.

In Aesop's Fable of the Tortoise and the Hare, the hare becomes overconfident and later feels regret for his laziness when the tortoise wins the race. Similarly, teens may try to manipulate their guilt to evade responsibility, but parents should guide them toward reflection and self-improvement rather than relying on guilt trips.

During the teenage years, the focus should be on open communication and leading by example. Islamic principles should be communicated clearly to teens, emphasizing personal accountability to Allah, while avoiding emotional manipulation through guilt trips.

What's Helpful

Evaluating whether guilt is justified is essential, especially in an Islamic context. When you reflect on your actions as a parent, ask yourself, "Does this feeling of guilt come from not fulfilling an obligation to Allah, or is it due to unrealistic expectations?" For example, a mother might feel guilty for not being able to provide expensive toys for her child, but upon reflection, she realizes that what matters most is raising her child with Islamic values. This helps her reframe the guilt as unjustified.

Striving to be a good parent, following the Prophet's (peace be upon him) example, is a noble goal. The Prophet Muhammad (peace be upon him) treated children with kindness, mercy, and patience. A real example of this is when a mother like Fatima remains calm after her child accidentally breaks a vase. Instead of reacting with anger, she follows the Sunnah by explaining to her child why they should be careful and gently guiding them toward rectifying the mistake. This way, she models the prophetic approach to parenting.

Another key principle is refusing to be swayed by guilt trips. For instance, if your teenage daughter, Aisha, insists that all her friends are allowed to stay out late, but you maintain a curfew based on Islamic guidelines, you can calmly explain, "Our family follows the principles of Islam, and staying out late exposes us to unnecessary risks." This shows Aisha that, while you empathize with her desires, you won't compromise on what is right. You're teaching her that standing by Islamic values is more important than yielding to emotional pressure.

Practicing self-forgiveness is crucial. Allah, the Most Forgiving, tells us in the Quran: "And whoever does a wrong or wrongs himself but then seeks forgiveness of Allah will find Allah Forgiving and Merciful." (Surah An-Nisa, 4:110). If you've made a mistake as a parent—like raising your voice in frustration—seek forgiveness from Allah and strive to do better next time. Reflect on how Allah's forgiveness can inspire you to be merciful to yourself.

Teaching your child to make amends helps them internalize the concept of repentance. A scenario could be if your son, Hamza, took his friend's toy without asking and broke it. Instead of only reprimanding him, you guide him towards taking responsibility by helping him apologize and offering to replace the toy. This aligns with Islamic values and teaches children that making amends is part of seeking forgiveness.

Maintaining boundaries even in the presence of guilt is vital. For example, if your daughter, Maryam, tries to manipulate you by saying, "You never let me do anything!" in response to a rule you've set, you can calmly explain, "I understand you feel upset, but our family has rules, and they are meant for your safety and well-being." This teaches children that just because they feel guilty or upset, it doesn't mean they should overstep established boundaries.

Encouraging your child to follow Islamic moral guidance sets a foundation for their spiritual and emotional well-being. When your child makes a mistake, instead of simply punishing them, use it as an opportunity to teach them about the importance of following Allah's guidance. For example, when your son, Abdullah, tells a lie, explain to him that honesty is a fundamental value in Islam, and guide him towards repentance.

Modeling sincere apologies is also crucial. In the Sunnah, the Prophet (peace be upon him) taught the importance of humility and rectifying wrongs. If you, as a parent, make a mistake—such as unjustly blaming your child for something—apologizing to them teaches them that everyone, even adults, can seek forgiveness and rectify their mistakes. This is not only a powerful teaching moment but also shows your child the beauty of accountability in Islam.

What's Not Helpful

Trying to be a perfect parent is an unrealistic goal that can lead to unnecessary guilt. In Islam, we are taught to strive for excellence, but perfection belongs to Allah alone. For example, a mother who constantly berates herself for not being able to do everything perfectly may feel drained and anxious. Instead, it's more helpful to focus on doing your best, trusting that Allah rewards sincere efforts.

Comparing yourself to others is also damaging. If a father constantly compares his parenting to other families who appear more affluent or more "put together," he will likely feel inadequate. It's important to remember that every family has its own struggles, and Allah has blessed each family in different ways. Reflect on the hadith: "Look at those below you and not at those above you, as it is more suitable to avoid belittling Allah's blessings." (Sahih Muslim). This hadith teaches that comparison detracts from gratitude.

Punishing yourself for mistakes isn't productive either. For example, if a mother feels guilty for accidentally missing a school event due to work commitments, instead of internalizing the guilt, she can make it up by spending quality time with her child later. This teaches that guilt should lead to positive change, not self-punishment.

Assuming guilt always means wrongdoing can distort your perspective. Sometimes, you might feel guilty because of external pressures rather than true fault. For instance, a father may feel guilty for not allowing his child to attend certain events that don't align with Islamic values. It's important to evaluate whether this guilt is justified or whether it stems from societal expectations.

Giving in to guilt to alleviate your feelings often leads to poor decisions. For example, if a parent feels guilty for disciplining their child and then compensates by buying them gifts, it sends mixed messages. Instead, it's better to stay consistent with discipline while balancing it with love and understanding.

Shaming your child instead of guiding them towards repentance and self-correction can damage their self-esteem and lead to deeper issues. For instance, if a parent constantly berates their child for making mistakes, the child may internalize these negative messages. Instead, use mistakes as teaching moments. For example, when your son, Bilal, forgets to pray, rather than shaming him, remind him gently of the importance of Salah and encourage him to seek forgiveness from Allah and strive to be better.

Chapter 4

What Is Emotional Self-Awareness?

Emotional self-awareness involves recognizing the emotions one is experiencing, identifying the triggers behind them, and understanding the impact of these emotions on others. Developing emotional self-awareness allows children to pause and reflect before reacting impulsively. A prime example of this is Aesop's fable of The Fox and the Grapes. In this story, the fox, after being unable to reach the grapes, convinces himself that they are sour and not worth having. This is a lesson in how emotions like disappointment can distort our perceptions. Children can be taught, through this fable, the importance of acknowledging their feelings of frustration or disappointment, rather than allowing these emotions to cloud their judgment or turn into bitterness.

An Islamic teaching that mirrors this comes from the story of Prophet Yusuf (peace be upon him). When faced with immense betrayal by his brothers, he did not allow anger or bitterness to dictate his actions but instead turned to Allah for strength and guidance. This kind of emotional intelligence helps children understand that emotions like anger or frustration should not control their behavior.

Modern therapy techniques such as ACT's "Passengers on the Bus" metaphor teach a similar concept. In this metaphor, emotions like anger, fear, or disappointment are seen as passengers on a bus that the individual is driving. Although one cannot control who gets on the bus (what emotions arise), one can control how to react and manage those passengers. This technique helps children understand the need to acknowledge emotions while not allowing them to steer their actions, aligning closely with Islamic values of self-restraint and discipline.

Emotional Regulation

A widely known proverb states: "He who angers you controls you." This reflects the importance of emotional regulation as a fundamental aspect of emotional self-awareness. By teaching children to identify and recognize their emotions and their triggers, they can avoid being controlled by these emotions.

CBT offers a technique known as Cognitive Restructuring, which can help children reevaluate their thoughts and emotional responses. This approach is similar to Islamic teachings on managing one's emotions and focusing on positive thought patterns. When children experience anger or frustration, CBT techniques can guide them to question whether their emotional reactions are helpful or productive. Combining this with Islamic practices such as dhikr (remembrance of Allah) and salah can reinforce emotional regulation.

Islamic literature, such as Stories of the Prophets by Ibn Kathir, published by Darussalam, presents narratives of various Prophets who exhibited exemplary emotional self-awareness and control. For instance, Prophet Musa (peace be upon him) demonstrated immense patience and self-control when dealing with the challenges posed by his people. This shows children that emotional intelligence fosters patience, self-discipline, and resilience.

Teaching Emotional Self-Awareness

A proverb often cited is: "The first step toward change is awareness." This resonates strongly with the need to teach emotional self-awareness to children. When children are able to recognize and name their emotions, they are in a better position to respond thoughtfully rather than impulsively.

The ACT metaphor of "Leaves on a Stream" provides a valuable teaching tool in this regard. Children are encouraged to visualize their emotions as leaves floating down a stream—passing by, rather than being something they must cling to or control. This helps children recognize that emotions are temporary and do not require immediate action. Similarly, Islamic teachings encourage mindfulness and the practice of reflection (tafakkur) to help manage emotional responses and avoid impulsive reactions.

Emotional awareness can enhance both personal and spiritual growth. Another famous fable, The Tortoise and the Hare, teaches a similar lesson: the hare, overconfident and arrogant, allows his emotions to lead to his downfall, while the tortoise, aware of his limitations, perseveres and succeeds. This is a classic example of how emotional self-awareness helps children manage their emotions and make better decisions in life.

Islamic Perspective on Emotional Intelligence

Islamic teachings provide a wealth of examples of how emotional intelligence is deeply embedded in the faith. For example, Umm Salamah (may Allah be pleased with her), who experienced deep grief after the death of her husband, turned to Allah for solace through the supplication taught by Prophet Muhammad (peace be upon him). This reflects how emotional self-awareness, combined with trust in Allah, can help manage intense emotions such as grief.

The ACT metaphor of "The Tug of War with a Monster" can also be applied here. The monster symbolizes negative emotions like grief or anger, and the more we struggle against these emotions, the stronger they become. By releasing the need to fight these feelings and turning to Allah, one can find peace. This aligns with Islamic teachings on the importance of emotional control and surrender to Allah's wisdom, which are key in managing challenging emotions.

Abu Bakr (may Allah be pleased with him) exemplified emotional intelligence throughout his caliphate. He faced numerous challenges with composure, emotional awareness, and a deep connection to Allah, demonstrating that emotional self-awareness is not just mental discipline but also spiritual practice. This mirrors modern psychological research, such as that found in CBT and ACT, which emphasizes mindfulness and emotional regulation to build resilience and enhance well-being.

Consider the fable of the Boy Who Cried Wolf. The boy repeatedly lies about a wolf attacking his flock, delighting in the emotional reactions of others. However, when a real wolf eventually appears, no one believes him. This story emphasizes the importance of emotional integrity and self-awareness. Had the boy understood the emotional consequences of his actions, he might have refrained from lying, recognizing that his deceit would harm others in the long run.

In a real-life example, imagine a mother named Layla, struggling to manage her emotions after the loss of a loved one. Without emotional self-awareness, her grief might cause her to withdraw or lash out, negatively affecting her relationship with her children. However, by recognizing and understanding her emotions, Layla could turn to Islamic practices of patience, prayer, and reflection to manage her grief more healthily, similar to how Umm Salamah (may Allah be pleased with her) navigated her loss.

The ACT metaphor of "The Observer" can aid in Layla's emotional regulation. In this metaphor, individuals are encouraged to step back and observe their emotions from a distance rather than being consumed by them. This perspective aligns with Islamic teachings on mindfulness and emotional control, allowing Muslims to approach life's trials with strength and grace, while placing trust in Allah's wisdom.

Lectures by Sheikh Abdul-Muhsin Al-Qasim frequently address these themes, emphasizing that emotional regulation combined with trust in Allah enables Muslims to face life's challenges with resilience and faith. Teaching emotional self-awareness within an Islamic framework equips children to be both emotionally intelligent and spiritually strong, grounding their emotional development in both modern therapeutic techniques and their faith in Allah.

Mastering the Parts of Emotional Self-Awareness

Emotional self-awareness is crucial for navigating life's challenges and is deeply connected to Islamic teachings. This skill includes three main components: identifying and labeling emotions, understanding the triggers behind emotions, and recognizing how one's emotional reactions affect others. Mastery of these components is vital for effective emotional management and fostering positive relationships in line with Islamic values.

Step One: Identifying and Labeling Feelings

Consider six-year-old Ahmad, who is bullied at school. Ahmad may experience a range of emotions such as anger, embarrassment, fear, or sadness. For instance, if Ahmad has been bullied before and struggles with making friends, he might feel sadness and isolation. If he values his peers' acceptance and fears exclusion, he might experience embarrassment, especially if the bullying occurs publicly. If Ahmad has been taught to assert himself, he might react with anger. In this case, let's say Ahmad feels scared due to the physical size difference between him and his bullies.

From an Islamic perspective, helping children identify and label their emotions is essential. The Prophet Muhammad (peace and blessings be upon him) showed deep empathy in dealing with emotional matters. For example, when a young boy mourned the loss of his pet bird, the Prophet (peace be upon him) comforted him and allowed him to express his grief. Similarly, parents should assist their children in naming their emotions, fostering understanding and acceptance rather than suppression.

The importance of acknowledging and addressing one's emotions.

This aligns with guiding children like Fatimah, who has recently moved to a new school and feels lonely. Her parents help her articulate these feelings, identifying them as loneliness and rejection, which is a foundational step toward emotional intelligence.

Step Two: Understanding What Caused the Emotion

While bullying may trigger Ahmad's fear, exploring deeper causes is crucial. Ahmad's fear might be due to concerns about physical harm or social exclusion rather than just the teasing. His fear could be linked to past experiences, such as previous bullying or witnessing aggression. Each child's emotional response is shaped by their unique experiences and values.

Islam encourages reflection on the causes of emotions for better management. Understanding the root cause of our emotions helps us approach challenges with sabr (patience) and tawakkul (trust in Allah).

In "Stories of the Prophets" by Ibn Kathir, the trials faced by Prophet Yusuf (peace be upon him) and his steadfast patience provide insight into managing deep emotional responses. Similarly, Bilal, a boy who becomes angry when criticized by classmates, might discover his anger stems from a need for respect. By understanding this root cause, Bilal realizes his emotional response is linked to his values of dignity and respect. He can then manage his reactions in line with Islamic teachings on humility and forgiveness, as demonstrated by the Prophet Muhammad (peace and blessings be upon him).

The saying, "Know thyself," underscores the importance of understanding the root causes of one's emotions. This proverb aligns with the concept of exploring and understanding emotional triggers to manage them effectively.

Step Three: Understanding How Your Emotions Affect Others

Ahmad's response to bullying—such as looking away and retreating to his teacher—might seem appropriate but could unintentionally reinforce the bully's behavior. The bully might perceive Ahmad's visible fear as a sign of weakness, leading to more harassment. Teaching children to recognize how their emotional reactions influence others is crucial for developing emotional intelligence.

From an Islamic perspective, controlling one's emotions is key to maintaining harmony and preventing conflicts. The Prophet Muhammad (peace and blessings be upon him) advised, "Do not become angry," highlighting the importance of self-control when provoked (Sahih al-Bukhari). Children should learn to respond with calmness and strength to prevent escalation.

Managing one's reactions to maintain social harmony.

For instance, when Ali is teased by friends, he calmly walks away rather than reacting with anger or fear. This response can defuse the situation and prevent it from worsening. Ali's behavior reflects prophetic teachings on restraint and wisdom. By understanding how his emotional response could escalate or de-escalate a situation, Ali aligns his behavior with Islamic principles of patience and forbearance.

In "The Tortoise and the Hare," the hare's impatience and arrogance lead him to underestimate the tortoise, whose steady and thoughtful approach ultimately wins the race. This story illustrates how one's emotional reactions and behaviors can affect outcomes and interactions with others.

Modern therapies such as Acceptance and Commitment Therapy (ACT) and Cognitive Behavioral Therapy (CBT) provide valuable tools for emotional self-awareness that resonate with Islamic teachings.

ACT Metaphor: "Passengers on the Bus"

In ACT, the "Passengers on the Bus" metaphor depicts emotions like fear, anger, or sadness as passengers on a bus we are driving. While these emotions may come and go, we, as the drivers, remain in control of the bus's direction. This metaphor teaches that while emotions are natural, they should not dictate our actions. In an Islamic context, this can be applied by teaching children that although emotions are inevitable, they should not control their behavior. Instead, they should use their emotional awareness to guide their actions in a way pleasing to Allah.

For instance, Mariam, who feels anxious about her schoolwork, learns to view her anxiety as a "passenger on the bus." Instead of letting her anxiety dictate her actions, she remembers she controls the bus and chooses to act with patience and trust in Allah. This approach strengthens her emotional resilience and aligns her responses with Islamic values.

CBT Technique: Thought Records

CBT uses thought records to identify and challenge negative thought patterns. For example, Ahmad might document his fears and associated thoughts, such as "I'm not safe" or "I will always be bullied." By examining these thoughts, Ahmad can challenge their validity and replace them with balanced, realistic thoughts, such as "I can seek help and protect myself."

Applying this within an Islamic framework involves reflecting on how these thoughts align with trust in Allah and teachings of patience. For example, Bilal might use a thought record to manage his anger, reminding himself of the Prophet's teachings on controlling one's emotions and responding with patience.

Incorporating mindfulness techniques from modern therapies can also be beneficial. Mindfulness helps individuals stay present and manage emotional reactions effectively. In an Islamic context, mindfulness aligns with being aware of Allah's presence during prayer (salah) and throughout daily life. Teaching children mindfulness techniques, such as deep breathing or focused attention, helps them manage emotions in a manner consistent with Islamic teachings.

Emotional expression, from an Islamic perspective, reflects personal growth and one's alignment with the teachings of Allah, the Most High. This expression manifests through verbal and nonverbal communication. Nonverbal cues, which include body language, eye contact, facial expressions, and tone of voice, account for over 90% of emotional expression. Verbal communication usually focuses on seven basic emotions: happiness, surprise, anger, fear, sadness, frustration, and disgust. These emotions vary in intensity, such as the difference between mild irritation and intense rage.

Islamic Foundations of Emotional Expression

Islam teaches that emotional control is part of good character and a sign of obedience to Allah. In a Hadith, the Prophet Muhammad (peace and blessings be upon him) said: "The strong person is not the one who can overpower others; rather, the strong person is the one who controls himself when he is angry" (Sahih al-Bukhari, Hadith 6114). Emotional mastery is viewed as the hallmark of true strength, reflecting discipline in the face of challenges.

This was embodied by Umar ibn al-Khattab (may Allah be pleased with him), a key figure in Islamic history, known for controlling his emotions even when provoked. When insulted in public, Umar responded with composure, demonstrating an Islamic approach to emotional regulation. His reaction serves as a powerful example of how restraint in anger aligns with Allah's teachings.

Similarly, in Acceptance and Commitment Therapy (ACT), emotions are seen as transient. A metaphor used in ACT compares emotions to weather patterns: clouds come and go but never last forever. Muslims practicing mindfulness and reciting Quranic verses can process their emotions effectively, using their faith as a means of grounding themselves in turbulent times.

Congruence Between Verbal and Nonverbal Emotional Expression

Emotional congruence, or the alignment of verbal and nonverbal expressions, is critical for effective communication. In cases where the two are not aligned, such as when someone says "I'm fine" but exhibits frustration through crossed arms and a frown, confusion can arise.

In Surah Al-Isra (17:53), Allah instructs believers: "And say to My servants to speak that which is best. Indeed, Satan induces dissension among them. Indeed, Satan is ever, to mankind, a clear enemy." This emphasizes the importance of genuine communication. The goal is to match one's verbal and nonverbal cues to foster harmony, thereby preventing misunderstandings.

Family Dynamics and Emotional Expression

Families significantly influence how children express their emotions. For example, studies in Asian cultures have shown that certain emotions, like anger or sadness, are discouraged, often leading to emotional suppression. This is reflected in Dr. Kazuo Murakami's work on stress, which explains how emotional suppression can lead to chronic stress and detachment.

Islamic teachings advocate for a balanced expression of emotions. The Prophet Muhammad (peace and blessings be upon him) wept openly at the loss of his son, Ibrahim, demonstrating that expressing grief is natural and healthy. His actions encourage Muslims to acknowledge emotions like sorrow, showing that emotional expression contributes to psychological well-being.

Avoidance of Verbal Emotional Expression

Many people avoid verbal emotional expression because of cultural influences or childhood conditioning. A study in Australia revealed that emotional suppression in Aboriginal communities stems from intergenerational trauma, with emotions like anger often being expressed through nonverbal cues instead.

In Islam, addressing emotions openly is encouraged, but with wisdom and control. A historical example highlights how the Prophet Muhammad (peace and blessings be upon him) responded calmly to a Bedouin who angrily demanded repayment of a debt. The Prophet's gentle manner and emotional restraint demonstrated the importance of acknowledging emotions while maintaining respect and wisdom.

Emotional Expression and Human Survival

Emotions serve a vital role in human survival, being integral to decision-making and self-preservation. In Maasai culture, for example, fear drives warriors to act in defense of their community when threatened by external dangers. This natural emotional response reflects the survival function of emotions and their role in social cohesion.

From an Islamic perspective, the Prophet Muhammad (peace and blessings be upon him) reminded believers to show mercy, particularly toward children. His teaching that "He is not of us who does not show mercy to our young ones" (Sunan Abi Dawood, Hadith 4943) highlights the importance of responding to children's emotional needs. Doing so ensures their emotional development and fosters strong relationships, both of which are crucial for long-term well-being.

Guiding Children Towards Healthy Emotional Expression

Addressing children's emotional needs from an Islamic perspective fosters their emotional resilience. Studies from developmental psychology emphasize the importance of bonding during early life, showing that responsive parents help build their children's emotional security. A father who listens and validates his child's frustration instead of dismissing it strengthens their problem-solving abilities and emotional intelligence.

For instance, a father in North America observed his son, Bilal, growing frustrated with a puzzle. By validating his son's feelings and encouraging him to keep trying, he reinforced Bilal's resilience, showing that healthy emotional expression can lead to growth, just as the Prophet Muhammad (peace and blessings be upon him) guided others through their emotional struggles.

Addressing Children's Fears

Children's fears evolve as they grow, and addressing them with patience and wisdom is essential. For instance, a case study from Brazil examined how children's fears shifted over time. Families who addressed their children's emotional concerns, supported by religious beliefs, saw better emotional outcomes.

In an Islamic example, a mother taught her daughter, Aisha, who was afraid of the dark, to recite Ayat al-Kursi before bed. This Quranic recitation not only calmed Aisha but also reinforced her belief in Allah's protection, instilling both emotional and spiritual resilience.

In guiding children through their fears, Islamic teachings provide a powerful source of comfort and reassurance. By turning to Allah and the Quran, children can develop a sense of security rooted in their faith. This practice also strengthens their emotional development, helping them process fear in a healthy manner.

Acceptance and Commitment Therapy (ACT) offers a metaphor that can be integrated with Islamic teachings. It compares emotions to waves in the ocean—sometimes they are large and overwhelming, but eventually, they subside. Similarly, teaching children to view their fears as temporary helps them gain perspective and trust in Allah's protection. This approach encourages them to accept their emotions rather than suppress them, fostering emotional growth and resilience over time.

The Role of Doctors' Advice in Emotional Health

Medical research and psychological studies have extensively examined the effects of emotional expression on health. According to Medscape, chronic suppression of emotions can lead to a variety of physical ailments, including cardiovascular disease and immune system dysfunction. Emotional regulation is crucial not only for mental health but also for overall physical well-being.

Doctors and psychiatrists often emphasize the importance of acknowledging emotions rather than bottling them up. Unexpressed emotions can manifest as physical symptoms over time.

Additionally, research in psychiatry textbooks underscores the link between emotional suppression and the onset of psychiatric conditions such as depression and anxiety disorders. Emotional suppression, particularly in childhood, can lead to difficulties in emotional regulation later in life, making it important for parents to foster healthy emotional expression in their children. Encouraging verbal and nonverbal emotional expression helps children develop emotional intelligence, equipping them with tools to navigate complex emotions throughout their lives.

The Impact of Emotional Expression on Community Well-Being

In Islam, emotional expression extends beyond the individual to affect the community at large. Emotional intelligence and healthy emotional regulation contribute to building strong, harmonious communities. When individuals communicate their emotions openly and sincerely, they foster understanding and empathy among family members, friends, and neighbors.

The Quran emphasizes the importance of unity and cooperation within the community: "Hold firmly to the rope of Allah all together and do not become divided" (Surah Al-Imran, 3:103). This unity is reinforced through emotional congruence and clear communication. When individuals openly express their emotions in a respectful and constructive manner, it fosters a culture of trust and mutual respect, which is essential for the well-being of the entire community.

Emotional expression, when guided by Islamic teachings, becomes a pathway to personal growth and social harmony. The Quran and Sunnah provide timeless wisdom on emotional regulation, encouraging believers to embrace their emotions while maintaining control over their actions. Combining this spiritual guidance with insights from medical and psychological research offers a comprehensive approach to emotional health that benefits both the individual and the broader community.

Teaching children to express their emotions appropriately within an Islamic framework is crucial for their emotional and spiritual development. This approach combines Islamic values with modern psychological insights, ensuring children grow up emotionally balanced and spiritually aware. Parenting in Islam involves patience, wisdom, and consistent guidance to help children communicate their feelings in ways that are pleasing to Allah, the Most High.

Case Scenario: Ayesha's Tantrum

Ayesha, a four-year-old, becomes furious when her younger brother takes her favorite toy and reacts by screaming and throwing things. Instead of responding with frustration, Ayesha's mother gently approaches her and says, "Ayesha, I know you're upset because your brother took your toy, but remember that Allah loves those who are patient. Let's calmly ask him to return it." This response not only addresses Ayesha's immediate frustration but also introduces key Islamic values like patience and emotional self-control.

The Prophet Muhammad (peace and blessings be upon him) encouraged gentle correction and teaching, rather than reacting with anger or impatience. Parents are advised to model these values in their interactions with their children, reflecting the approach of Ayesha's mother, who exemplifies these teachings in guiding her daughter.

This scenario mirrors techniques in Acceptance and Commitment Therapy (ACT), where children are encouraged to accept their emotions and commit to actions based on values such as kindness and patience. Islamic teachings similarly emphasize acting according to virtues like sabr (patience) and rahmah (mercy), even in challenging situations.

Labeling Emotions in an Islamic Context

Helping children label their emotions aids their emotional development and helps them communicate their feelings more effectively. From an Islamic perspective, this practice also helps children connect their emotions to their spirituality. For instance, when a child feels guilty after missing a prayer, a parent might say, "I feel sad because

I missed salah today, and it reminds me to strive harder in worshipping Allah."

Islamic Historical Example:

The Prophet Muhammad (peace and blessings be upon him) taught that emotions such as sadness and grief should be acknowledged but always within the bounds of submission to Allah. When the Prophet wept at the death of his son Ibrahim, he acknowledged his grief but reminded people not to say anything displeasing to Allah during such times. This example shows how to balance emotional expression with spiritual consciousness.

Modern psychiatry also utilizes emotion labeling in Cognitive Behavioral Therapy (CBT) to help individuals process emotions thoughtfully. This practice aligns with the Islamic practice of mindfulness in emotional expression.

Nonverbal Expression and Islam

Nonverbal communication, such as facial expressions, body language, and tone of voice, is essential for expressing emotions. In Islam, nonverbal communication is also significant, as the Prophet Muhammad (peace and blessings be upon him) emphasized good manners, empathy, and kindness. A simple smile, as taught by the Prophet, is considered an act of charity.

Though Umar (Allah be pleased with him) was known for his strength, he was often moved to tears during moments of reflection on Allah's greatness. This example demonstrates that emotional vulnerability and strength can coexist, reflecting humility and spiritual awareness.

In Gems and Jewels by Darussalam, stories of the Sahabah (companions) illustrate how nonverbal cues such as tears and facial expressions were used to convey emotions like awe, fear, and love for

Allah. These examples teach children that emotions should be expressed in a way that aligns with their faith.

Medical and psychiatric textbooks emphasize the importance of nonverbal communication in emotional regulation. Techniques such as deep breathing and posture adjustments can help manage emotions, aligning with Islamic teachings of calm and mindful behavior.

Helping Children Understand and Manage Emotions

As children grow, their emotional responses become more complex. Parents must help them manage these emotions in ways consistent with Islamic teachings. For instance, when a child refuses to sleep because they want to continue playing, a parent might explain, "I see that you want to keep playing, but rest is important for your health, and Allah loves those who take care of their bodies."

Scenario: Ahmed's Fear of the Dark

Ahmed, a five-year-old, is afraid of the dark. His mother reassures him, saying, "It's okay to feel afraid, Ahmed, but remember that Allah is always with us, even in the dark. Let's ask Him for protection." This statement helps Ahmed embrace his fear while fostering a sense of tawakkul (trust in Allah). Islamic teachings encourage reliance on Allah in moments of fear and anxiety, similar to psychological therapies that help children cope with anxiety by fostering safety and trust.

Ali's Grief

Ali, an eight-year-old, is grieving the death of his pet cat. His father comforts him by saying, "I know you are sad, but remember that Allah gives life and takes it away. We must trust in His wisdom." This helps Ali process his grief while connecting it to Islamic concepts of life and death. Similarly, CBT encourages reframing thoughts to find comfort and meaning in difficult emotions.

Helping Children Manage Emotions According to Islamic Teachings

Modeling emotional regulation is key to helping children manage their emotions in a manner consistent with Islamic principles. By demonstrating calm behavior and providing reminders of Islamic values, parents can guide children to respond to anger, sadness, and frustration with patience, gratitude, and remembrance of Allah.

Scenario: Sarah's Hurt Feelings

Sarah, a ten-year-old, accidentally spills milk in class and is teased by her classmates. Her teacher says, "I know it hurts when others tease you, Sarah, but remember that our worth is determined by how Allah sees us, not by others. Let's be patient and forgive those who hurt us." This reinforces the Islamic teaching of forgiveness, as mentioned in Surah Al-Imran (3:134), where Allah praises those who restrain their anger and forgive others. In psychiatric therapy, fostering forgiveness and self-worth is used to help children manage hurtful experiences, aligning with Islamic teachings on emotional regulation.

In Patience and Gratitude by Ibn Qayyim al-Jawziyyah, published by Darussalam, the value of sabr (patience) is emphasized in dealing with emotional challenges. This book encourages parents to teach their children patience and forgiveness, reflecting on how these values are key to emotional and spiritual growth.

Aesop's Fable: The Tortoise and the Hare

This fable teaches about perseverance and not letting frustrations lead to giving up. Just as the tortoise remains steady despite challenges, children can learn to handle their emotions with patience and determination.

African Proverb:

"Smooth seas do not make skillful sailors." This proverb highlights that facing and managing difficult emotions can build resilience, much like navigating rough seas helps sailors become more adept.

Allowing Children to Have Their Feelings

In Islamic teachings, acknowledging and understanding children's emotions is crucial for their emotional and spiritual development. Just as adults may perceive the same situation differently—one person may feel cold while another feels warm—children also experience and react to emotions uniquely. Allowing your child to have their feelings and recognizing that their emotions are valid and personal to them is essential for fostering emotional intelligence and spirituality.

Examples and Case Scenarios:

For example, consider a child named Fatimah who struggles with frustration. If Fatimah shows anger towards her newborn sibling, it might be tempting to downplay her feelings by saying, "You know you love your little sister. Be nice to her." However, Fatimah may not yet feel affection for her new sibling and could be experiencing resentment due to changes in family dynamics and reduced time with you. Ignoring or minimizing her feelings might reinforce her anger and erode her trust in you as someone who understands and accepts her emotions.

In another scenario, think of three-year-old Ibrahim. During a visit to a friend's house, Ibrahim's parents give significant attention to their baby and engage in play with him. If Ibrahim shows frustration or anger due to feeling neglected, it is crucial to address his feelings with empathy and guidance. Instead of dismissing his emotions, Ibrahim's parents should acknowledge his feelings and help him understand and manage them. This approach aligns with the teachings of patience and empathy in Islam.

Modern Therapeutic Insights:

Acceptance and Commitment Therapy (ACT) emphasizes that emotions should be accepted rather than fought against. For instance, if Fatimah feels anger and left out because of her new sibling, ACT would recommend acknowledging her feelings without judgment and finding ways to help her engage in meaningful activities that align with her values, such as spending quality time with family members. This approach encourages her to accept her emotions while finding constructive ways to address them.

Cognitive Behavioral Therapy (CBT) focuses on helping individuals reframe their thoughts about situations. For example, if Ibrahim feels neglected, CBT might involve guiding him to identify and challenge distorted thoughts, such as believing that his parents don't care about him. By reframing these thoughts, Ibrahim can develop healthier perspectives and coping strategies.

Self-Help and Psychological Insights:

In The Whole-Brain Child by Daniel J. Siegel and Tina Payne Bryson, the authors emphasize the importance of validating children's emotions and using strategies that integrate emotional and cognitive development. They recommend techniques like "name it to tame it," where children are encouraged to verbalize their feelings to better understand and manage them.

Research in developmental psychology, such as studies published in Developmental Psychology and reported on Medscape, shows that children who receive emotional validation from their caregivers tend to develop better emotional regulation skills and have improved social outcomes. For instance, a study highlighted in Medscape emphasizes that emotional validation helps in reducing behavioral issues and enhancing social competencies in children.

Medical and Psychiatric Insights:

Textbooks such as Developmental and Behavioral Pediatrics by William Carey discuss the importance of acknowledging children's emotions in fostering healthy psychological development. The book highlights that dismissing or minimizing a child's emotions can lead to issues with emotional regulation and behavioral problems later in life.

In Child Psychiatry and the Law by Robert A. Dineen, the author explains how validating children's feelings is crucial in therapeutic settings. This book provides case studies illustrating how emotional validation can lead to better outcomes in therapy by helping children develop a more robust sense of self and better coping strategies.

The life of the Prophet Muhammad (peace and blessings be upon him) offers valuable lessons in managing children's emotions. For example, during prayer, his grandsons Hasan and Husayn (Allah be pleased with them) played on his back. Instead of reprimanding them, the Prophet showed patience and kindness, demonstrating the importance of understanding and managing emotions with compassion. This example underscores the significance of addressing children's feelings with empathy and understanding.

Similarly, the story of Prophet Yunus (peace be upon him) in the belly of the whale illustrates the importance of patience and turning to Allah during times of emotional distress. Despite his difficult situation, Prophet Yunus sought solace in Allah with unwavering trust, exemplifying the value of patience and faith during emotional struggles.

Aesop's Fable: "The Lion and the Mouse"

In this fable, a tiny mouse helps a mighty lion, and the lion later repays the kindness. This story highlights the idea that even small, seemingly insignificant actions can have significant emotional impacts. Just as the lion accepted the mouse's help, children benefit from having their feelings acknowledged, regardless of how small they may seem.

"The Tortoise and the Hare"

In this tale, the slow and steady tortoise wins the race against the swift hare. The story illustrates the value of persistence and self-acceptance, encouraging children to understand their unique qualities and emotions, rather than feeling pressured to conform.

North American Native Tale: "The Story of the Two Wolves"

In this tale, a grandfather tells his grandson about the two wolves inside him—one representing positive traits and the other negative. The story illustrates the importance of understanding and managing one's emotions to foster a positive and balanced life.

Listening to a child's emotions can sometimes be challenging and evoke strong feelings in you. To support your child effectively, prepare yourself to be an attentive and empathetic listener. Utilize modern therapeutic insights, such as ACT and CBT, as well as medical and psychiatric knowledge to better understand and address your child's emotions. Seek support from your spouse, a trusted friend, or an Islamic counselor if needed. This practice aligns with the Islamic principle of seeking knowledge and support from knowledgeable and trustworthy sources. The Prophet Muhammad (peace and blessings be upon him) encouraged seeking advice and support in various aspects of life, including managing personal and familial challenges. This guidance ensures that both you and your child navigate emotional difficulties in a manner consistent with Islamic teachings and modern therapeutic practices.

As the family was about to head home from a busy day out, baby Aisha started to fuss and cry. The father quickly began changing Aisha's diaper while the mother packed up their belongings. Yusuf, feeling upset, approached his father and said, "Dad, why don't we return Aisha to the place where we got her? It seems like she's always needing attention now." The father looked at Yusuf and replied, "Yusuf, it sounds like you're feeling a bit frustrated with having to share my attention with Aisha." Yusuf remained silent, listening. His father continued, "I know it's different now, and it's harder to find time for just us like before Aisha was born. But I care deeply for both you and Aisha, and we're not going to separate from either of you." With that, the father embraced Yusuf warmly. Yusuf's feelings of frustration began to ease as he felt his father's understanding and love. This acknowledgment of Yusuf's emotions helped him feel more at ease and connected. Recognizing and validating a child's feelings is crucial in helping them navigate and manage their emotions effectively. Ignoring or dismissing their feelings rarely resolves the underlying issue.

Modern Therapeutic Approaches

Modern therapeutic approaches reinforce this principle. Acceptance and Commitment Therapy (ACT) uses the metaphor of "The Bus," which represents how individuals can allow their thoughts and emotions to be passengers on the bus of their life, without allowing them to steer the vehicle.

Similarly, Cognitive Behavioral Therapy (CBT) employs tools like "Thought Records" to help individuals identify and challenge negative thoughts that contribute to emotional distress.

An effective approach for helping children express their feelings is to teach them to use "I" statements. These statements are structured to convey emotions clearly and respectfully: "I feel (emotion) because (what happened to upset me)." This method not only helps children articulate their emotions but also fosters open and respectful communication, aligning with Islamic teachings that emphasize empathy and understanding.

For example, consider little Ibrahim, who feels frustrated because his older sister Fatima has taken the book he was reading. Ibrahim might express his feelings by saying, "I feel frustrated because you took my book without asking." This approach mirrors the Prophet Muhammad's (peace be upon him) practice of addressing children's feelings with kindness and respect. The Prophet Muhammad (peace be upon him) demonstrated a deep understanding of children's emotions.

Similarly, if young Maryam is feeling lonely because her mother is doing Haj, she might say, "I feel lonely because Mommy is not here with me."

In another scenario, when older Yusuf feels apprehensive about participating in a new school play, he might say, "I feel nervous because I'm unsure if I will perform well."

From a common-sense perspective, if a child named Sara is upset because her friend Ahmed accidentally bumped into her while playing, she might say, "I feel upset because you bumped into me and it hurt." This simple approach helps Sara communicate her feelings without assigning blame, promoting understanding and reconciliation. This mirrors the Prophet Muhammad's (peace be upon him) practice of addressing misunderstandings with clarity and kindness, as seen in his interactions where he would gently correct misunderstandings and promote harmonious relations.

Similarly, if little Hasan is feeling scared about starting a new school, he might say, "I feel scared because I don't know what to expect." This expression helps Hasan share his anxieties openly, facilitating support and reassurance from his parents or teachers. The Prophet Muhammad (peace be upon him) encouraged addressing fears with compassion and reassurance, as reflected in his teachings and interactions with his companions and family, where he provided comfort and guidance to those in distress.

Modern therapeutic approaches also endorse the use of "I" statements to help children manage their emotions. Acceptance and Commitment Therapy (ACT) utilizes metaphors like "The Bus," where individuals visualize their thoughts and emotions as passengers on a bus, allowing them to be present without steering the direction of their lives. This metaphor helps children accept their feelings without letting them dominate their actions.

These "I" statements, supported by both Islamic teachings and modern therapeutic techniques, assist children in articulating their emotions clearly and respectfully. This approach fosters constructive communication and emotional regulation, reinforcing the values of empathy and understanding as emphasized by the Quran in Surah Al-Ankabut (29:69): "And those who strive for Us - We will surely guide them to Our ways." This guidance includes effectively addressing and managing emotions, reflecting both traditional and contemporary practices in promoting emotional well-being.

Chapter 5

In Islam, noble education requires vigilant supervision and adherence to high moral standards. Fathers, mothers, and teachers play a vital role in guiding children and preventing harmful behaviors:

1. Lying: Lying is considered one of the most objectionable traits in Islam. Parents must closely monitor their children's honesty and actively teach them about the negative impacts of lying. The Prophet Muhammad (peace be upon him) emphasized this by advising against lying to children, even in minor situations. For example, Abu Dawud narrates that 'Abdullah Ibn Amir said, "One day my mother called me while the Messenger of Allah was with us. She said, 'Come and take this!' The Prophet asked her, 'What are you intending to give him?' She replied, 'Dates.' The Prophet warned, 'Beware, if you do not actually give him anything, it would be considered a lie.'" Ahmad reported that the Prophet said, "If anyone says to a child, 'Come and take this,' but does not actually give it, this is a clear lie."

- If a parent promises their child a special outing for good behavior and then fails to follow through, it can lead to disappointment and mistrust. This can teach the child that promises are not important, encouraging them to break promises as well.

- If a parent tells their child, "I'll be right back," but takes much longer than expected without informing the child, it can cause anxiety and undermine the child's trust in the parent's reliability.

- If a parent says, "I'm too busy right now, maybe later," but never follows up, the child might learn to disregard promises or excuses, leading to a habit of dishonesty.

2. Theft: Theft is a serious issue and can be prevalent in environments lacking strong moral guidance based on Islamic principles. Parents should instill a sense of religious observance and fear of Allah, along with an understanding of the consequences of theft in this world and the Hereafter. Extreme cases illustrate the severity of this issue. For instance, a young boy sentenced to have his hand cut off for theft said, "Before you cut my hand, cut off my mother's tongue. My first theft was picking up an egg from a neighbor's house. My mother didn't scold me; she even praised me, saying, 'Praise be to Allah! My son is now a man!' Without her encouragement, I would not have become a thief."

- If a child takes a toy from a sibling without permission and the parents ignore it or reward the child for taking the toy, it can teach the child that theft is acceptable. Addressing the behavior immediately and explaining why it is wrong helps the child understand respect for others' belongings.

- If a child is caught taking a small item from a store without paying and the parents dismiss it or downplay its seriousness, the child might not grasp the gravity of theft and may repeat the behavior.

- If a child finds and keeps a lost item without trying to return it to its owner, and the parents praise the child for keeping the item, it can reinforce the idea that taking what does not belong to them is acceptable.

3. Abuses and Insults: Abusive language and insults are often learned from adults or peers. Parents should model respectful behavior and shield their children from negative influences. They should teach their children about the importance of avoiding offensive language, using Hadith as guidance. Al-Bukhari and Muslim report, "Abusing a Muslim is an immoral act, and fighting against him is disbelief." The Prophet Muhammad (peace be upon him) also warned against cursing

one's parents, explaining that such behavior usually starts with insults toward others, leading to further abuse.

- If a child hears their parents using harsh language or insults during disagreements, they might mimic this behavior in their own interactions with others, believing it is acceptable.

- If a child observes their parents making derogatory comments about others, the child may adopt a similar attitude and use offensive language themselves.

- If a child sees their parents using sarcasm or ridicule in daily conversations, the child might learn to communicate in a hurtful way, affecting their relationships with peers and family members.

- If a child is exposed to verbal aggression in the home, they may become desensitized to abusive language and may use it in their interactions with friends or in school.

By maintaining consistent supervision and setting a positive example, parents can effectively prevent these issues and foster noble behavior in their children.

4. Indulgence and Dissolution: This behavior has become increasingly prevalent among today's youth, both boys and girls, largely due to their exposure to social media. They often become drawn toward corruption and immorality, viewing life as an opportunity for immediate pleasure, shamelessness, and lawless activities. For them, missing out on such behaviors can make life seem meaningless. The Messenger (peace and blessings of Allah be upon him) offered practical principles and righteous guidelines for steering children towards upright behavior and true Islamic morals.

Among these principles are:

i. Warning Against Blind Mimicry

The Prophet Muhammad (peace and blessings of Allah be upon him) emphasized the importance of distinguishing oneself from non-Muslim practices. Al-Bukhari and Muslim report that the Prophet (peace and blessings of Allah be upon him) said, "Behave differently from the atheists by shaving the mustache and keeping the beard," and "Cut off the moustache, and keep the beard, and thus be different from the Magians." As reported by At-Tirmidhi, the Hadith states, "Anyone of us who adopts the dress of others is not one of us; do not wear the dress of Jews or Christians." Another Hadith from At-Tirmidhi advises, "Do not be an opportunist who says, 'I will follow the behavior of those around me; if they do good, I will follow; if they behave badly, I will do the same.' Instead, develop the habit of doing good if others do good, and avoid their misbehavior if they act poorly."

In modern society, many parents take pride in their children imitating dialogues from popular movies or performing scenes and dances inspired by Western culture. There is a trend to view such behavior as "cool," while those who refrain from these activities might be labeled as outdated or narrow-minded.

- Imitating Movie Scenes: If a child frequently mimics dialogues or behaviors from movies or TV shows with inappropriate content, and parents see this as amusing or harmless, it can lead the child to internalize those behaviors and values.

- Adopting Popular Trends: If a child starts following every trend promoted by social media, such as fashion or lifestyle choices that contradict Islamic principles, and parents encourage or ignore these choices, it can lead the child to value societal approval over moral integrity.

- Celebrating Non-Islamic Holidays: If parents allow or encourage their children to participate in non-Islamic celebrations and customs, viewing them as entertaining or trendy, it may cause the child to devalue their own religious traditions and practices.

- Conforming to Peer Pressure: If a child is influenced by peers to engage in activities contrary to Islamic teachings, and parents do not address these influences or provide guidance, the child might view such behaviors as acceptable for social acceptance.

- Inappropriate Language and Behavior: If parents permit their child to use inappropriate language or engage in improper behavior because it is popular or seen as trendy, without correcting it, the child may come to view such behavior as normal and acceptable.

By setting clear boundaries and offering guidance rooted in Islamic principles, parents can help their children navigate these challenges and maintain a strong moral compass.

ii. Forbidding Excessive Enjoyment

The divine guidance reminds us that, "Thereafter, indeed you will be definitely questioned about bliss." Additionally, Mua'z Ibn Jabal cautioned, "Beware of excessive enjoyment, for the true worshippers of Allah do not indulge in excessive enjoyment."

In two authentic Hadiths, 'Umar Ibn Al-Khattab wrote to the Muslims in Persia, advising, "Beware of excessive enjoyment and the garbs of polytheists." Here, excessive enjoyment refers to an overindulgence in luxuries and pleasures, which can lead one away from true devotion and balance in life.

Many parents today focus on allowing their children to experience unrestricted pleasure without considering the moral implications. This can include permitting activities like dancing, watching inappropriate content on TV, or mingling freely with the opposite gender, without distinguishing between what is right and wrong.

- Indulgence in Luxuries: If parents continuously provide their children with luxury items and expensive toys, without teaching them the value of moderation and gratitude, it can lead to a sense of entitlement and lack of appreciation.

- Unsupervised Socializing: Allowing children to freely interact with the opposite gender or participate in mixed-gender activities without supervision or clear boundaries can lead to inappropriate behavior and confusion about appropriate social interactions.

- Overindulgence in Food and Treats: Constantly giving children access to excessive amounts of sweets or fast food without teaching them about balanced eating can promote unhealthy habits and a lack of self-control.

- Celebrating Non-Islamic Festivals: Encouraging participation in non-Islamic holidays or cultural practices that involve excessive enjoyment and activities contrary to Islamic teachings can undermine a child's understanding and adherence to Islamic values.

By setting appropriate boundaries and fostering a balanced approach to enjoyment, parents can guide their children towards a more meaningful and disciplined way of life.

iii. Music and Singing

The Prophet (peace and blessings of Allah be upon him) predicted in a Hadith, as narrated by Al-Bukhari, Ahmad, and Ibn Majah, that a time would come when some people from his nation would consider adultery, the wearing of silk, drinking wine, and playing music permissible, despite their clear prohibitions in Islam.

In another Hadith, reported by At-Tirmidhi from Abu Musa, the Prophet (peace and blessings of Allah be upon him) said, "Anyone who listens to songs will not be allowed to listen to the rauhaneein (the reciters of the Quran) in the Garden." This warning highlights the potential harm of music and singing, as it often leads to indulgence in forbidden behaviors, such as immorality, excessive luxury, and heedlessness toward religious obligations.

- Avoiding Music at Social Gatherings: Muslim families who host gatherings refrain from playing music and instead create an atmosphere of remembrance of Allah by playing Quranic recitations, fostering a spiritually uplifting environment.

- Choosing Islamic Education Over Entertainment: Parents who encourage their children to listen to Islamic lectures or Quranic recitations rather than music help cultivate an attachment to Islamic values and limit the potential influence of harmful content.

- Avoiding Music During Daily Routines: Muslims who make a conscious effort to avoid listening to music while driving, exercising, or working ensure their time is spent in a way that pleases Allah, such as engaging in dhikr or reflecting on His blessings.

- Limiting Exposure to Social Media: Muslim families actively monitor and stop their children's use of social media to prevent exposure to music videos and content that contradicts Islamic teachings, encouraging them to follow Islamic scholars and learn beneficial knowledge.

- Choosing Islamic Alternatives: Muslim parents who introduce their children to lectures, provide wholesome entertainment aligned with Islamic principles, avoiding the negative influences of mainstream music.

iv. Dressing, Speaking, and Acting Like the Opposite Gender

The Prophet (peace and blessings of Allah be upon him) strongly emphasized maintaining the distinctions between genders, as highlighted in authentic Hadiths.

In a Hadith, narrated by Al-Bukhari, Abu Dawud, and At-Tirmidhi, Ibn Abbas reported that the Prophet (peace and blessings of Allah be upon him) cursed men who acted effeminately and women who displayed virility. Islam promotes the preservation of clear gender roles, as altering them can lead to confusion and a weakening of moral and societal structures. Moreover, the Prophet (peace and blessings of Allah be upon him) forbade men from wearing silk and gold, which are adornments reserved for women, emphasizing the need to maintain gender distinctions.

Teaching Gender Roles Through Islamic Traditions: Muslim parents who instill Islamic values in their children teach them the importance of adhering to their respective gender roles, encouraging modesty and appropriate behavior according to Islamic teachings.

- Avoiding Gender-Confusing Fashion Trends: Muslim families who choose clothing that aligns with Islamic principles avoid gender-neutral fashion trends and ensure that boys and girls dress according to the standards of Islamic modesty, reinforcing their unique roles.

- Encouraging Respectful Speech: Parents who teach their children to speak in a manner befitting their gender, encouraging boys to use respectful and assertive speech and girls to speak with modesty and dignity, help reinforce gender identity in line with Islamic values.

- Providing Role Models: Muslim families who introduce their children to role models from Islamic history, such as male Prophets like Ibrahim and Musa or female leaders like Maryam and Khadijah, help instill a strong sense of gender identity through examples of noble men and women.

- Avoiding Trends that Blur Gender Lines: Muslims who resist societal pressures to adopt behaviors or clothing that blur the lines between genders reinforce the importance of maintaining the distinctions that Islam upholds, strengthening both personal and community identity.

By nurturing Islamic values and adhering to the guidance of the Prophet (peace and blessings of Allah be upon him), Muslims can help safeguard their communities from the confusion and moral challenges that arise from neglecting the clear distinctions between the sexes and indulging in music and other forbidden activities.

v. Unveiling, Flaunting, Intermixing, and Forbidden Viewing

Allah the Most High commands in the Quran:

"O Prophet! Tell your wives, your daughters, and the believing women to draw their cloaks (veils) over their bodies. This is better, so they may be recognized (as honorable and free women) and not be harassed. Allah is Ever-Forgiving, Most Merciful." (Al-Ahzab: 59)

Allah also instructs both men and women to observe modesty:

"Tell the believing men to lower their gaze (from looking at forbidden things) and protect their private parts (from unlawful acts). That is purer for them. Verily, Allah is All-Aware of what they do. And tell the believing women to lower their gaze and protect their private parts, and not to expose their adornment except that which necessarily appears thereof. And let them draw their veils over their bosoms and not expose their adornment except to their husbands..." (An-Nur: 30-31)

Regarding flaunting, Allah commands:

"And stay in your homes and do not display yourselves as was the display of the times of ignorance." (Al-Ahzab: 33)

In a Hadith recorded by Imam Muslim, Abu Hurairah reported that the Prophet (peace and blessings of Allah be upon him) said:

"There are two types of people of Hell whom I have not yet seen: people with whips like the tails of cows with which they beat people, and women who are dressed but appear naked, swaying and causing others to sway. Their heads are like camels' humps. These people will not enter Paradise nor even smell its fragrance, though its fragrance can be perceived from a great distance."

Prohibition of Intermixing

Allah commands gender separation to preserve the purity of the heart, saying:

"And when you ask them (the Prophet's wives) for something, ask them from behind a screen; that is purer for your hearts and their hearts." (Al-Ahzab: 53)

The Prophet (peace and blessings of Allah be upon him) also warned against seclusion between men and women. In a Hadith narrated by At-Tirmidhi, the Prophet (peace and blessings of Allah be upon him) said:

"Let no man be alone with a woman, for the third one present is Satan."

In another Hadith from As-Sahihayn, the Messenger of Allah (peace and blessings of Allah be upon him) said:

"Beware of entering places where women reside!" When asked if this applies to in-laws, the Prophet (peace and blessings of Allah be upon him) replied: "The in-laws are death."

Furthermore, Imam Muslim narrates that the Prophet (peace and blessings of Allah be upon him) said when asked about an unintended glance:

"Turn your gaze away."

- Observing Hijab: Women should consistently wear the hijab and dress modestly, fulfilling the command of Allah and avoiding exposure that could lead to harassment. This commitment to modesty reinforces their status as honorable believers and protects their dignity. Implementing this in daily life involves choosing modest clothing in public, covering appropriately in front of non-mahrams, and being mindful of how one presents herself in various settings.

- Lowering the Gaze: Muslim men and women should practice lowering their gaze in situations where they might be tempted to look at something inappropriate, whether in person or through media. This includes in workplaces, public areas, or online interactions. By constantly remembering this command, Muslims can protect their hearts from sinful desires and foster purity. For instance, if encountering someone not related to you in public, a conscious effort is made to look away, fulfilling the command of Allah.

- Avoiding Mixed Gatherings: Families should seek to avoid gatherings where men and women freely intermingle in social settings. This can be implemented by organizing gender-segregated events for weddings, social functions, and family gatherings. Muslim homes can also maintain clear boundaries for guests of the opposite gender, ensuring that interactions remain respectful and within Islamic guidelines.

- Maintaining Gender Separation in Mosques: Mosques should ensure that men and women have separate prayer spaces. This allows worshipers to concentrate fully on their connection with Allah without the distraction of the opposite gender. Mosques can implement this by having designated entrances, prayer areas, and guidelines for both genders to maintain modesty and decorum.

- Teaching Modesty to Children: Parents should instill the values of modesty in their children from a young age by setting clear boundaries regarding dress, behavior, and interaction with others. This involves encouraging them to adopt Islamic attire, teaching the importance of lowering their gaze, and ensuring that boys and girls understand the need for separation in certain situations, such as when playing or attending events. Implementing this could include encouraging children to avoid mixed-gender parties and fostering environments that promote respectful interaction.

- Maintaining Privacy and Avoiding Seclusion: Muslims should be mindful of situations where they might find themselves alone with someone of the opposite gender who is not their mahram. This can be implemented by ensuring that workplaces, social gatherings, and everyday interactions avoid such scenarios. If a situation arises where one might be alone with someone of the opposite gender, efforts should be made to leave the situation or include others, avoiding the risk of temptation.

Through these practices, Muslims can implement the commands of Allah in their daily lives, preserving modesty, dignity, and the purity of their hearts while building a society rooted in Islamic principles and morality.

Importance of Divine Principles for Societal Well-being

When Muslim communities adhere to Divine principles such as modesty, gender separation in social settings, and refraining from forbidden behaviors, they naturally cultivate a society grounded in purity and virtue. This results in peace, security, and well-being, both in this world and the Hereafter. Parents and educators play a critical role in instilling these principles, which form the foundation of ethical conduct, personal morality, and good manners as prescribed by Islam.

However, the heavy responsibility lies on us as parents and educators to closely observe our children's upbringing. If we examine the causes of moral decline and deviant behavior in children, we often find that it stems from our neglect to properly educate and guide them in accordance with Islamic values, thereby betraying the trust Allah has placed in us.

Allah is Always Watching

One of the essential lessons to teach children is the constant awareness that Allah is always watching them. This awareness can be nurtured by reminding children that Allah knows their every action, their innermost thoughts, and even their secrets. As Allah says in the Quran:

"He knows the treachery of the eyes and what the breasts conceal." (Ghafir: 19)

By instilling this consciousness in children, we help them develop sincerity in all their deeds and words, knowing that Allah accepts only actions done purely for His sake. Teaching them to constantly remember Allah will train them to reflect on their actions and think about their intentions, fostering self-awareness and accountability. This awareness will ultimately help them reach the level of Ihsan—worshipping Allah as though they see Him, knowing that even though they do not see Him, He sees them.

1. Incorporating Taqwa (Awareness of Allah) into Daily Life: Parents can regularly remind their children that Allah is always present, even when no one else is watching. For example, if a child is tempted to take something that doesn't belong to them, parents should gently remind them that Allah sees everything. This instills honesty and nurtures a conscience based on the constant remembrance of Allah.

2. Creating Boundaries in Social Interactions: In homes and communities where clear gender boundaries are maintained during

gatherings, schools, or community events, the atmosphere remains modest and free from temptation. Muslim families, for instance, should ensure that gatherings are gender-segregated to maintain Islamic values and foster an environment where both boys and girls grow up with respect for each other's modesty.

3. Teaching Modesty from a Young Age: Parents can instill a love for modesty in their children by teaching them the significance of proper dress and behavior. For example, girls are encouraged to wear hijab once they reach maturity, and boys are guided to dress modestly. This practice helps Muslim children internalize modesty as a core part of their identity, preventing them from seeking validation through immodest actions as they grow older.

4. Establishing Daily Rituals of Salah and Dhikr: Families can foster spiritual growth by establishing daily prayers together, making it a habit for children to pray the Sunnah prayers with their parents and Fard prayers together in the Mosque. By observing Salah, children develop a natural connection to Allah. For instance, parents who wake their children for Fajr create a sense of discipline and help them appreciate the blessings of beginning their day in the remembrance of Allah.

5. Setting Positive Role Models through Conduct: Children learn by example. When Muslim parents actively demonstrate Islamic values, such as lowering their gaze, avoiding inappropriate interactions, and speaking with kindness, they serve as role models. A mother who wears the hijab and conducts herself with dignity in public sets an example for her daughters, while a father who shows respect toward women sets a precedent for his sons.

Implementing Divine Principles in Real Life

To implement these Divine principles in real life, Muslim families should begin with cultivating a home environment centered on Islamic teachings. This includes regular discussions on modesty, respect, and the importance of gender boundaries in social interactions. By integrating lessons of Allah's watchfulness into daily routines, children develop a deeper connection to their faith and a strong moral compass.

For example, Muslim parents can encourage children to reflect on their actions each night before bed, reminding them of Allah's constant presence. Establishing regular family prayers strengthens the bond of faith and instills discipline. Additionally, ensuring that family gatherings, weddings, and community events uphold Islamic principles of gender separation and no photography and vidography helps normalize modest behavior and reinforces the importance of Islamic teachings in public settings.

When implemented in daily life, these principles lead to personal growth, stronger family bonds, and the cultivation of a community that lives in harmony with the guidance provided by Allah. Such a society not only enjoys peace and security but also prospers spiritually, fulfilling the purpose of being created to worship Allah in sincerity.

Causes of Children's Deviation

A significant factor contributing to a child's deviation from Islamic principles is parental negligence, particularly when fathers fail to closely monitor the influences and activities surrounding their children. When a father neglects to ensure that his children avoid the company of immoral or unprincipled individuals, he risks allowing them to adopt harmful behaviors and attitudes. The importance of cultivating relationships with righteous friends cannot be overstated, as bad company can lead to the erosion of a child's moral values.

Similarly, when a father permits his children to watch mobile or TV, he inadvertently guides them toward spiritual harm. Such exposure can numb their sensitivity to sinful behavior and plant the seeds of violence and indecency in their hearts.

Allowing children access to immoral content, whether through magazines, books, or websites, is another way parents may unintentionally contribute to their children's moral decline. Without proper guidance, children can easily fall into bad habits and harmful behaviors that are difficult to correct.

Furthermore, a father who is indifferent to his wife's and daughters' observance of hijab, or who fails to prevent them from mingling with inappropriate company, risks the loss of their modesty and dignity. When children, particularly daughters, are not guided to uphold Islamic values, they may become vulnerable to dishonorable conduct. By the time regret sets in, the damage may be irreversible.

Fathers must also take an active role in supervising their children's personal activities and belongings. Children who collect indecent images, read inappropriate materials, or engage in flirtatious communication require strict supervision and guidance. Without proper parental oversight, they may be led astray by the temptations of modern culture, further distancing themselves from Islamic values.

1. Monitoring Friendships and Social Circles: Muslim parents should be vigilant about their children's social interactions. For example, organizing regular family visits to righteous friends' homes or Islamic events at the mosque can ensure that children are surrounded by peers who share and reinforce Islamic values.

2. Controlling Media Consumption: Fathers should set clear guidelines for media consumption, which is not to allow the children to watch anything unsupervised, that is when they are alone. For instance, a father might designate specific times for watching Islamic documentaries together, or listening to Quran recitations together as

a family, thereby creating a wholesome and spiritually enriching environment.

3. Encouraging Beneficial Reading: Parents can promote a love for reading by introducing their children to age-appropriate Islamic literature, such as stories of the Prophets and books on Islamic manners. This encourages children to seek knowledge that strengthens their faith and character, rather than being drawn to harmful or trivial content.

4. Promoting Modesty in Dress and Behavior: Fathers who emphasize the importance of modesty in both dress and behavior help their families adhere to Islamic principles. For example, taking the time to discuss the significance of hijab and the virtues of modesty with daughters can instill a deep respect for these values, making them less susceptible to societal pressures. After children understand that Islam is the truth and all its commands and prohibitions are for their own good, they will happily follow all the teachings of Islam and even guide their friends towards the truth.

5. Supervising Personal Activities: Regularly reviewing children's online activities, personal belongings, and communication is essential. A father might check his older child's social media usage if such usage is required by his school or university (otherwise normally in children there should be no social media usage) and discuss any concerns, reinforcing the importance of using these platforms responsibly and in line with Islamic teachings.

6. Creating a Righteous Environment at Home: Parents can establish a home environment that reflects Islamic values, such as displaying Islamic calligraphy, maintaining cleanliness, and ensuring that family conversations are respectful and free from gossip or backbiting. This instills a sense of Islamic identity and pride in children.

7. Engaging in Family Worship: Encouraging children to participate in daily prayers and other acts of worship as a family fosters a strong connection with Allah. For example, parents can lead by example, performing Sunnah Salah together at home and making dua with their children, which helps them internalize the importance of worship. All the members of the family can do the morning and evening remembrances together at the same time although each recites these supplications separately.

8. Addressing Inappropriate Behavior Immediately: When parents observe any inappropriate behavior or deviation from Islamic norms, it is crucial to address it promptly and with wisdom. For instance, if a child is caught watching inappropriate content, a father might explain why it is harmful and offer alternative, halal entertainment options.

9. Incorporating Islamic Lessons in Daily Life: Parents can teach children Islamic principles through everyday activities. For example, involving children in charitable acts, such as distributing food to the needy or donating to a mosque, can reinforce the values of compassion, generosity, and community responsibility.

10. Open Communication and Trust-Building: Establishing open lines of communication where children feel comfortable discussing their challenges and experiences is vital. A father might schedule regular one-on-one conversations with each child, discussing their day and addressing any concerns or questions they have about Islam or life in general.

By implementing these practical measures, Muslim parents can effectively guide their children towards righteousness, ensuring they grow up grounded in Islamic values and protected from the influences that lead to deviation. This proactive approach not only nurtures their spiritual and moral development but also contributes to the overall well-being of the Muslim community.

Managing Behaviors: Helping Muslim Children Express Their Emotions

Imagine your child, Fatimah or Abdullah, says, "I'm upset." What should happen next? After acknowledging their feelings, it is essential to guide them in processing these emotions in a healthy, Islamic manner. Many Muslim parents may unintentionally suppress their child's feelings, unsure of how to guide them. However, the prophetic Sunnah teaches us the importance of accepting and validating emotions. Once their emotions are acknowledged, it is crucial to offer constructive and halal outlets for them, ensuring these outlets adhere to Islamic principles.

Handling Anger in an Islamic Way

For Muslim children of all ages, there are several Islamic methods to help them manage their anger. Here are ten real-life examples:

1. Drawing or Journaling: Encourage your child to express anger through drawing or journaling. For instance, Fatimah can draw a picture of what upset her, allowing her to channel her emotions creatively and safely. Similarly, Abdullah can write about his feelings, much like a letter he never sends, allowing him to reflect on his anger without resorting to harmful behavior.

2. Designated Quiet Space: Establish a calming area in your home filled with Islamic books, where your child can retreat when feeling overwhelmed. For example, when Abdullah is upset, he knows to go to his designated spot to recite Quran or make dua, helping him connect with Allah and find peace.

3. Physical Activity: Physical activities such as kicking a soccer ball or taking a walk can help children release their frustration in a halal way. For instance, Ahmed may take a walk with his parent or play in the yard

after feeling angry, helping him calm down and handle his emotions more appropriately.

4. Dhikr and Reflection: Encourage your child to engage in dhikr when they are upset. For example, Maryam can sit quietly and recite "SubhanAllah" or "La ilaha illallah" when she feels anger rising. This helps her refocus and remember the importance of patience (sabr) in Islam.

5. Problem-Solving Discussion: Once your child has calmed down, have a conversation with them about their feelings. For example, after Fatimah has had time to reflect, her parent can sit with her and discuss how to address similar situations in the future, teaching her the importance of problem-solving with Islamic guidance.

6. Teaching Positive Communication: In the case of younger children, Ahmed or Maryam can be taught to express their anger calmly. For instance, when upset with a sibling, they can be guided to say, "I feel angry because..." This helps them communicate their feelings without shouting, in line with the Prophet's (peace be upon him) gentle manner of addressing conflicts.

7. Modeling Behavior: As parents, it is important to model how to handle anger in an Islamic way. When Abdullah sees his father calmly making wudu (ablution) after getting upset, he learns the value of this prophetic method for cooling down and purifying the heart.

8. Engaging in Prayer: Teach your child to offer two rak'ahs of salah when feeling angry. For example, Fatimah might step away to pray and ask Allah for patience and guidance, following the practice of turning to salah in times of distress.

9. Physical Comfort: Sometimes children simply need a physical reminder of their parents' love. For example, if Ahmed is angry, his mother might hold him and let him calm down in her arms. This

simple act of affection helps the child feel secure, easing their frustration.

10. Storytelling with Islamic Teachings: After your child has calmed down, tell them stories of the Prophets and companions who exemplified patience and good character in difficult times. For instance, Maryam can hear about the patience of Prophet Musa (peace be upon him) in the face of adversity, learning that controlling one's anger is a strength admired by Allah.

Handling Tantrums with Wisdom

If your child throws a tantrum in public, respond calmly by removing them from the situation. For example, if Ahmed begins a tantrum at the store, take him to the car or an empty corner, allowing him time to cool down. This communicates that such behavior is not acceptable and that he will not get his way through an outburst. At home, a tantrum can be ignored until it naturally subsides, reinforcing patience and Islamic manners in handling disappointment. Once calm, discuss the feelings that led to the outburst and use the opportunity to teach Islamic lessons on controlling one's temper and avoiding selfishness.

Teaching Respectful Anger Toward Authority

Anger toward authority figures like parents, teachers, or elders is a natural emotion. Instead of discouraging this feeling altogether, teach your child that while anger is normal, it must always be expressed respectfully within Islamic boundaries. For example, Fatimah may be upset with her teacher, but her parents can remind her to express her feelings respectfully. They might say, "It's okay to feel upset, but you must use kind words and good manners when speaking to your teacher, just as the Prophet (peace be upon him) showed respect even when addressing difficult situations."

By teaching children that respect and dignity are core Islamic values, even in moments of disagreement, parents help them grow into responsible and emotionally intelligent Muslims who reflect the character of the Prophet (peace be upon him) in their actions.

These examples demonstrate how integrating Islamic teachings with practical approaches can guide children in managing their emotions, ensuring they grow up with a balanced and righteous way of handling life's challenges.

Expressing Sadness: A Suitable Approach for Devout Muslims

Children often experience sadness, whether it's due to a beloved family member, such as Jannah's or Yusuf's aunt or uncle, leaving after a long visit, a parent traveling for work, the passing of a cherished pet, or the loss of a favorite toy. While it may be tempting for adults to ease this sadness with incentives like special outings, extra playtime, or new toys, it is crucial to approach sadness from an Islamic perspective.

The Islamic Perspective on Handling Sadness

Addressing sadness effectively rather than masking it with indulgences is important. When children experience sadness, it often impacts the emotions of caring adults as well. Temporarily alleviating sadness with rewards might feel comforting in the short term, but it prevents children from learning how to manage their emotions constructively. Instead of relying on material incentives, consider approaches that align with Islamic teachings and address sadness thoughtfully.

Constructive Approaches to Address Sadness

1. Storytelling with Islamic Lessons: Share stories from Islamic history about individuals who faced sadness and managed it with faith. For instance, recount the story of Prophet Ayub (peace be upon him) and

his patience through suffering. This teaches children that sadness is a natural experience and managing it with faith is a key Islamic principle.

2. Discuss Personal Experiences: Share your own experiences of dealing with sadness, highlighting how you relied on Allah and practiced patience. If your child, Aisha, is mourning the loss of a pet, tell her about a time when you experienced a similar loss and found comfort through prayer and remembrance of Allah.

3. Encourage Expression Through Writing: Allow your child to express their feelings by writing letters to departing family members or making lists about what they loved about the lost pet. This approach helps them process their emotions in a reflective manner, consistent with Islamic practices of thoughtful expression.

4. Family Rituals for Coping: Engage the family in honoring the memory of a lost pet or loved one. This reinforces family bonds and Islamic values while helping children cope with loss.

5. Acknowledgment of Feelings: Validate your child's feelings by acknowledging their sadness openly. For instance, if Fatimah is upset about her father's travel, simply recognizing her feelings with words like, "I see you miss Daddy a lot, and that's okay," helps her feel heard and supported. This method fosters emotional resilience in line with prophetic examples.

Additional Examples

1. Remembrance and Dua: Encourage your child to engage in dua and dhikr (remembrance of Allah) during moments of sadness. If Ibrahim is upset about losing a favorite toy, guide him to recite supplications like "Hasbunallahu wa ni'mal wakeel" (Allah is Sufficient for us and He is the Best Disposer of affairs), helping him find solace through remembrance.

2. Family Prayer Time: Use family prayer (salah) as a way to collectively address and process sadness. If Maryam feels distressed by changes in the family routine, come together for extra prayers and seek Allah's comfort and guidance as a family. This reinforces turning to Allah in times of difficulty.

3. Positive Reflection: Assist your child in reflecting on positive aspects and blessings. For example, if Zayd is disheartened by a canceled birthday party, encourage him to think about and list the blessings he has, such as family and friends, fostering a sense of gratitude and perspective.

4. Learning Through Islamic Stories: Read Islamic books or stories that deal with handling grief and sadness. For instance, share stories about the companions of the Prophet Muhammad (peace be upon him) who faced trials with faith. These narratives offer valuable lessons on managing emotions through trust in Allah.

5. Offering Comfort and Reassurance: Provide comfort that aligns with Islamic teachings. If Ahmed is anxious about a family member's illness, reassure him by reminding him of Allah's mercy and the importance of making dua for the sick, reinforcing trust in Allah's plan.

By incorporating these approaches, you help your child navigate sadness in a manner that reflects emotional maturity and adherence to Islamic principles.

Facing Their Fears: A Suitable Approach for Devout Muslims

When addressing situations that frighten your child, it is crucial to handle them with gentleness, respect, and reassurance. As children grow, their fears change. For example, a two-year-old might fear separation from their parent, a five-year-old might fear being in the dark, and a nine-year-old might be concerned about real threats such as the death of a parent or being kidnapped.

Understanding Fear and Anxiety

Anxiety is a generalized feeling of worry or tension without a specific cause or target, while fear is directed towards a specific person, animal, or thing, including imaginary things. Children often articulate their fears clearly when asked.

Strategies for Overcoming Fear

The approach to helping your child overcome fear depends on their age and the nature of the fear. Here are some methods, aligned with Islamic teachings and practices:

1. Gentle Reassurance and Respect: Address your child's fears with gentleness and respect. For instance, if Yasmine feels anxious about being apart from her father, preparation is key. Ease her anxiety by sending a family photo album with a note from you, having regular video calls, or preparing her favorite snacks to enjoy during your absence.

2. Gradual Exposure: For older children facing fears, gradual exposure can be effective. Take the example of seven-year-old Musa, who was once fearless about riding his bicycle but became afraid after a minor fall. His parents developed a plan to help him regain his confidence. They started by having Musa observe from a safe distance while they rode together. Gradually, they encouraged him to ride on a flat surface with support, offering praise and encouragement until he felt comfortable riding again.

3. Islamic Guidance and Patience: Encourage your child to seek comfort through Islamic practices. Teach them to recite protective supplications, such as the dua: "Bismillahi allathee la yadurru ma'asmihi shay'un fil-ardi wala fissama'i wa Huwas-Samee'ul-'Aleem" three times after the fajr and asr prayer (In the name of Allah, with whose name nothing on earth or in the heavens can cause harm, and

He is the All-Hearing, All-Knowing). This practice helps instill a sense of security and trust in Allah.

4. Positive Reinforcement and Support: Support your child with positive reinforcement. For example, if Amina is nervous about performing in a school play, start by having her practice her lines at home in front of the family. Gradually increase the audience size as she becomes more comfortable, celebrating her progress and providing encouragement in line with Islamic values of patience and perseverance.

5. Storytelling with Islamic Examples: Share stories from Islamic history that illustrate overcoming fears with faith. For instance, narrate the story of Prophet Ibrahim (peace be upon him) and his unwavering trust in Allah when he was thrown into the fire. This story demonstrates how strong faith and reliance on Allah can help overcome even the greatest fears and challenges.

6. Encouraging Independence: If your child, Ahmed, is afraid of starting a new school, help him adjust gradually. Begin by visiting the school together before the term starts. Let him explore the classrooms and meet his teacher. Gradually introduce him to new classmates during these visits to help him become more comfortable.

7. Using Islamic Rituals: If your child, Zainab, is afraid of loud noises such as fireworks, teach her to recite the dua for protection: "Allahumma inni a'udhu bika min sharri hadhihi al-mass" (O Allah, I seek refuge with You from the harm of this event). This practice helps her feel more secure and connected to Islamic teachings.

8. Seeking Community Support: If Bilal is apprehensive about joining a new sports team, involve supportive community members. Connect him with older children or friends who are already part of the team. Their positive experiences and encouragement can help ease his anxiety.

9. Modeling Calm Behavior: Show calmness when dealing with situations that may be frightening. If your child, Maryam, is anxious about visiting a new place, display composure and confidence. Your calm demeanor can help her feel more at ease and less fearful.

10. Gradual Introduction to New Experiences: For children like Yusuf, who may be nervous about attending a new event, introduce him gradually. If he is anxious about a family gathering, start by attending smaller gatherings and gradually increase the size of the events he participates in.

By implementing these strategies, you help your child navigate their fears with emotional maturity and adherence to Islamic principles, fostering resilience and trust in Allah's guidance.

Consider a scenario where you and your child, Amina, are preparing for a family gathering. You have selected a festive dress for Amina, but she protests because she prefers her everyday play clothes. Alternatively, as the weather gets cooler, you choose a warm sweater for her, but Amina insists on wearing a summer dress. Or perhaps you want Amina to wear a new outfit for a special occasion, but she resists because she wants to wear her favorite outfit, even though it's not suitable for the event. These scenarios are common as children develop their own tastes and preferences. It is normal for Amina to express strong opinions about her clothing.

To manage these situations effectively and avoid conflicts, you can adopt a more inclusive approach. For example, when choosing an outfit for a family event, pick two or three options that are appropriate for the occasion and according to the teachings of Islam, and then let Amina choose from these. This way, you ensure that the outfit is suitable while giving Amina a sense of control.

By offering Amina a selection of appropriate clothing options, you respect her preferences and create a positive environment, which helps in reducing potential conflicts over clothing. This approach not only fosters her sense of independence and self-expression but also ensures she adheres to suitable attire for various occasions.

Parenting a child can sometimes seem like the only word they know is "no." Your child, two years old, like little Mariam, is developing autonomy and expressing preferences, which is a healthy part of their growth. Balancing when to enforce rules and when to allow them to make choices can be challenging.

A practical rule to follow is to remember that if the issue involves safety or health, there is no room for negotiation. For example, if little Ibrahim refuses to wear his helmet while riding his bicycle, a firm but gentle response like, "Wearing the helmet is not optional," is necessary. You can empathize by saying, "I understand you don't like the helmet," or explain, "The helmet keeps you safe," but be ready for continued resistance. In matters of safety, maintaining firmness is crucial.

Determining whether something is a safety issue can sometimes be complex. For instance, if Mariam, who loves climbing, decides to climb onto a high shelf, you need to assess the risk. Similarly, if she insists on running around the house in socks, despite the risk of slipping, but she manages to stay steady and enjoys it, weigh the risk versus her enjoyment and skill level. Safety must be a priority as your child grows. Strive to find solutions that encourage independence while ensuring safety. For instance, provide age-appropriate climbing toys, supervise her closely, and use non-slip socks.

Encouraging Independence with Patience

This principle also applies to other aspects of independence. Whether it's letting them feed themselves, choose their own clothes, or walk to the car instead of being carried, children often want to "do it myself." While it may test your patience to let a two-year-old, like Fatima, slowly try to put on her coat or struggle with buttons, these moments are important. Consider the long-term benefits of allowing them to practice these skills.

1. Performing Salah: If Amina wants to try performing Salah (prayer) on her own, even if it means she may not get all the movements perfectly, allow her to do so. This encourages her to take responsibility for her prayers and understand their importance in a hands-on way.

2. Islamic Dress Code: When getting ready for a family gathering or Islamic event, if Yusuf prefers to choose his own outfit, provide a few options that are suitable according to Islamic dress code. This respects his choice while ensuring he adheres to religious guidelines.

3. Contributing to Charity: Allow Mariam to select and pack items for charity, such as food or clothing donations. This teaches her about the importance of giving and fosters a sense of responsibility in helping those in need.

4. Learning to Read Quranic Verses: If Ibrahim wants to read Quranic verses by himself, let him practice, even if he makes mistakes. This encourages his interest in the Quran and helps build his independence in religious learning.

5. Managing Ramadan Fast: As Amina grows older and begins to understand fasting during Ramadan, let her manage her own schedule for Suhoor and Iftar, within safe limits. This encourages responsibility and a deeper commitment to the practice of fasting.

Give yourself this pep talk: "I will appreciate it later when my child completes their religious duties independently, manages their personal tasks, and makes thoughtful decisions. I'll be relieved when they trust their own judgment and act confidently. I'll be grateful when they engage in their Islamic responsibilities with sincerity and independence. Encouraging my child to be self-reliant now will build their confidence and independence for the future."

Remind yourself often during these early years. Though their path to independence can be challenging, nurturing a child's independence is a valuable investment in their future.

Independence develops across three crucial areas: physical, financial, and social-emotional. To ensure your child grows up well-rounded and capable in all these aspects, it is essential to provide them with opportunities to make decisions and practice independence in each of these areas.

Physical Independence: Encourage your child, like little Ahmed, to take on physical tasks on their own. For instance, let him dress himself or clean up after his meals. This approach builds self-confidence in his physical abilities and nurtures a sense of responsibility.

Financial Independence: As your child grows, begin teaching them foundational financial skills. For example, involve Sara in managing the family grocery budget or provide her with a small allowance to handle. This helps her grasp the value of money and understand financial responsibility.

Social-Emotional Independence: Support your child in developing social-emotional skills by allowing them to express their feelings, make decisions about their activities, and interact with others independently. For instance, let Abdullah choose which friends he wants to invite to a gathering or handle minor disagreements with his peers on his own. This aids in building emotional resilience and social competence.

Additional Examples:

Islamic Rituals: Allow little Aisha to make her own choices about which Islamic prayers to memorize, while offering guidance on the importance of these prayers. This fosters a sense of personal responsibility and commitment to her religious practices.

Participating in Family Decisions: Involve young Tariq in simple family decisions, such as choosing a family outing destination or selecting a dish for a special meal. This helps him feel valued and understand the importance of contributing to family decisions.

Managing Eid Preparation: As Amina grows, involve her in planning and preparing for Eid celebrations, such as selecting gifts for family members or organizing decorations. This encourages her to take initiative and responsibility for significant family events.

Volunteering Opportunities: Allow Mariam to choose which local charity or Islamic community service projects she wants to participate in. This promotes her sense of responsibility and compassion while aligning with Islamic values of charity and community service.

Islamic Study Sessions: Let Omar select and lead a small Islamic study group or Quranic study session with his peers. This encourages him to take ownership of his religious education and develop leadership skills within an Islamic framework.

Learning Islamic Practices: Allow Aisha to manage her own practice of Wudu (ablution) before prayers, even if it's not perfect. This encourages her to take responsibility for her religious cleanliness and understanding of prayer preparation.

Helping with Household Chores: Involve Tariq in age-appropriate chores, such as setting the table for meals or helping with simple cleaning tasks. This teaches him responsibility and the value of contributing to family life in accordance with Islamic principles of cooperation and service.

Managing Ramadan Fasting: As Amina matures, let her manage her own fasting schedule during Ramadan, including planning her pre-dawn (Suhoor) and evening (Iftar) meals with guidance. This builds her sense of responsibility and commitment to fulfilling her religious duties.

Choosing Islamic Books: Encourage Mariam to select her own Islamic books or stories for bedtime reading. This promotes her interest in Islamic knowledge and fosters independent learning while aligning with her religious upbringing.

Participating in Community Service: Let young Omar choose which charity or community service activities he wants to participate in. This encourages him to take an active role in helping others, fostering a sense of social responsibility and compassion in line with Islamic values.

By providing balanced opportunities for independence in these areas, you help your child develop a well-rounded ability to manage various aspects of life with confidence and responsibility, in alignment with Islamic teachings and principles.

When your child, such as little Amina, shares their daily experiences, use these moments to teach them assertiveness and discuss these situations with them. For example, you might ask, "How did you handle it when Hassan wanted to use your special notebook without asking?" If Amina refused and explained that the notebook is personal to her, praise her for setting a clear boundary. If she allowed Hassan to use it because she wasn't sure how to refuse, it's important to teach her assertive communication. Help her practice phrases such as, "I need to keep my notebook to myself because it's special to me," or simply, "No, I can't lend my notebook right now." Use concepts like "setting boundaries," "saying no," "expressing your opinion," and "standing up for yourself" to help her link her feelings with assertive actions and language.

As your child matures, they will encounter more opportunities to demonstrate assertiveness through their actions, not just words. For instance, a pre-teen like Omar who stands firm against friends trying to make him miss his prayers is demonstrating assertiveness. Similarly, a child who decides to avoid joining in with peers who are behaving inappropriately demonstrates assertiveness. A child who asks their teacher for clarification on a difficult Islamic studies topic shows assertiveness. Even a younger child like Fatima, who speaks up to an older cousin who is ignoring her while focused on their game, deserves recognition and support from her parents.

1. Respecting Personal Items: If little Aisha's friend wants to borrow her new pen without asking, teach her to say, "Please ask before using my pen. I like to keep it to myself." This helps her assert her ownership and personal space.

2. Addressing Inappropriate Comments: If Ahmed's classmates make unkind remarks about his religious practices, encourage him to respond with, "I don't appreciate those comments. Please respect my beliefs." This helps him assert his dignity and faith.

3. Declining Activities Against Beliefs: When Sara is asked to join an event that doesn't align with her Islamic values, guide her to say, "Thank you for inviting me, but I can't attend as it conflicts with my values." This helps her communicate her boundaries respectfully.

4. Ensuring Fair Assistance: If Tariq's older sibling is not helping him with his homework as they agreed, teach Tariq to say, "Please assist me with my homework as promised, or let me know if you need more time." This helps him assert his needs and expectations.

5. Seeking Guidance: If Fatima struggles with a challenging concept in her Islamic studies, encourage her to ask a knowledgeable adult, "Can

you help me understand this topic better? I'm having some difficulty." This demonstrates her initiative in seeking support.

Teaching assertiveness helps your child protect themselves from peer pressure, unwanted demands, and manipulation. It builds their self-confidence, allowing them to ask questions, express their opinions, and refuse unreasonable requests with conviction. Assertiveness reinforces a child's sense of self-worth and respect, emphasizing that it involves maintaining self-respect while also respecting others.

Chapter 6

Sarah and Tariq sought guidance for their fourteen-year-old son, Sami, because they were uncertain how to address his behavior. "He refuses to listen to us," Sarah explained. "He ignores our instructions and seems indifferent to our opinions." Tariq added, "I can't understand what has happened to our cherished son. We've provided him with everything he could ever want, and this is how he responds?"

Sarah and Tariq, older parents by most standards, had Sami when Sarah was forty and Tariq was forty-five. Sami was their "blessed" child. After nearly a decade of attempting to conceive and almost losing hope, Sarah became pregnant. From the moment he was born, Sami was the joy of their lives.

The family spent nearly all their time together. Whether they were attending the masjid, going on family outings, or spending time at home, they always catered to Sami's wishes. They provided him with all the material possessions he desired and allowed him to enjoy his childhood without many responsibilities, believing that he should solely focus on being a child.

Problems began when Sami turned twelve. He became increasingly rebellious and argumentative, and the conflicts with his parents intensified over the years. The situation became evident when they overheard one of Sami's classmates describe him as one of the "challenging boys" at school. This was a distressing revelation for Sarah and Tariq, as it meant their son's behavior was impacting others beyond their home.

Teachers and school staff had noticed Sami's behavior as well. His teachers reported that he was often disruptive in class, failed to complete assignments on time, and had difficulty working cooperatively with other students. The school counselor mentioned that Sami's attitude was affecting his academic performance and relationships with peers.

Sami's extended family, including his grandparents, Ahmed and Fatima, and his uncles and aunts, also observed his behavior during family gatherings. They were concerned that Sami's disrespectful attitude was influencing his younger cousins, who were beginning to mimic his behavior. Sami's uncles Ahmed Jr. and Bilal, along with his aunts Maryam and Aisha, offered support but were unsure how to effectively intervene.

Sami showed no desire to change, so if his parents wanted his behavior to improve, they needed to change their approach. Sarah and Tariq attended a counseling session without Sami to discuss strategies for helping their son.

The issues appeared to be:

1. Sami's Self-Centered Attitude: Sami had come to believe he was the center of attention due to his parents' excessive indulgence.

2. Lack of Social Skills: Sami struggled with social interactions because he lacked basic skills like empathy and sharing.

To support Sami effectively, Sarah and Tariq needed to make the following changes:

1. Set Clear Limits: This involved saying no and being consistent, even if Sami reacted negatively.

2. Allocate Time for Themselves: They needed to spend time apart from Sami, including time together as a couple, to show that their lives did not revolve around him.

3. Make Privileges Conditional: Instead of giving Sami everything he wanted regardless of his behavior, Sarah and Tariq needed to show him that privileges had to be earned.

Initially, Sarah said, "But we don't mind doing all these things for Sami. He's our only child, and we want to give him everything we can." It was emphasized that whether they "minded" or enjoyed doing nice things for their son wasn't the issue. It was harmful for Sami to receive unlimited attention and material possessions without any responsibilities.

After a thorough discussion about how their approach had led to the current situation, both parents acknowledged their role in shaping Sami's self-perception. They had treated him like a special prince, and over time, he began to believe he was the center of the universe.

Over the following weeks, Sarah and Tariq implemented stricter rules and assigned more responsibilities to Sami. They stopped showering him with praise and material goods, and for the first time, Sami had to complete chores to earn an allowance.

At first, his behavior worsened. He resisted and refused to cooperate. However, his parents remained firm. They shifted the focus away from Sami and required him to earn privileges based on good behavior. They emphasized the importance of kindness and stopped yielding to all his demands.

His grandparents and relatives noticed the shift and supported the new approach, helping reinforce the importance of respect and responsibility.

The school saw improvements as well. Sami's teachers reported better behavior and academic performance, and the school counselor noted a positive change in his interactions with peers. Sami's attitude gradually improved, and he began to take on responsibilities more willingly.

Sarah and Tariq understood that changing Sami's self-view wouldn't happen overnight. It had taken years for him to develop the belief that he was the center of attention, and it would take time to correct this misconception. Nonetheless, Sarah and Tariq were committed to making this change, as they didn't want their pampered teenager to become an irresponsible adult.

In line with Islamic teachings, it is crucial to avoid the misconception that providing your child with excessive material possessions makes you a better parent. Similarly, don't assume that giving your child more will naturally lead them to be more generous. Such approaches can actually be counterproductive.

Instead, focus on teaching your child the significance of contributing to society and helping others. Engage them in discussions about their potential to positively impact their community rather than concentrating solely on their future wealth or career success. For example, rather than stressing the importance of receiving numerous gifts during special occasions, encourage them to think about what they can offer others through acts of charity and kindness.

Here are practical ways to implement these principles in your life as a devout Muslim parent:

Encourage Charity (Sadaqah): Help your child understand the value of giving by involving them in charitable activities. For instance, you might involve them in organizing a community iftar during Ramadan or participating in a local charity drive. This teaches them to appreciate the joy of giving and the impact of their contributions on others.

Focus on Community Service: Instead of spending all your time managing extracurricular activities, allocate some of it to community service projects. For example, volunteer together at a local shelter or participate in neighborhood clean-up drives. This provides a practical lesson in contributing to society and helps your child see the importance of their actions.

Model Self-Care and Balance: Show your child the importance of balancing personal well-being with family responsibilities. Schedule regular time for activities that benefit you, such as attending religious classes, exercise, or hobbies. This balance demonstrates the importance of self-care and helps your child understand that maintaining personal interests is part of a healthy lifestyle.

Adhere to Fairness and Rules: Teach your child to respect rules by ensuring they follow the same standards as their peers. For example, if your child does not meet the criteria for a school club or sports team, support their acceptance of this and encourage them to work harder next time. Reinforce the Islamic principle of fairness by showing them that everyone must adhere to established rules.

Promote Responsibility: Involve your child in household chores and responsibilities, such as helping with meal preparations or managing their own schoolwork. This teaches them that privileges and comforts are earned through responsibility and effort, aligning with the Islamic teaching of personal accountability and diligence.

Teach Gratitude: Encourage your child to express gratitude for the blessings they have. For example, before a meal, have them say a prayer of thanks and reflect on the importance of appreciating what they have.

Involve Them in Family Decisions: Include your child in family discussions and decisions that affect them. For example, involve them in planning a family trip or budgeting for a family event. This helps them understand the importance of contributing to the family and making informed choices.

Encourage Volunteerism: Support your child's participation in volunteering opportunities within the local mosque or community center. For instance, they could help in organizing Quran classes for younger children or assist in mosque maintenance.

Set Clear Limits: Establish and enforce rules for behavior and privileges. For example, limit screen time or enforce study times with clear consequences for not following these rules. This teaches them about the importance of boundaries and accountability.

Foster a Spirit of Sharing: Encourage your child to share their belongings with others. For instance, if they have toys or books they no longer use, suggest donating them to less fortunate children. This teaches the value of generosity and caring for others.

By adopting these practices, you not only adhere to the Islamic values of justice and responsibility but also guide your child toward becoming a well-rounded, respectful individual, fulfilling the teachings of the Prophet Muhammad (peace be upon him).

Understanding the importance of relationships is crucial for success in various aspects of life. Forming a meaningful marriage, working effectively with a team, resolving conflicts with neighbors, and securing a first job all require strong relationship skills. Some children naturally develop these skills, possibly due to their outgoing nature or by learning from their parents' positive relationship behaviors. However, for children who are naturally shy, have not observed healthy relationships, or have not been taught effective relationship skills, the challenge can be more significant.

Interaction is essential for emotional well-being, and relationship skills are not innate for every child, especially those who are more introverted. It is crucial to offer these children ample opportunities to practice social skills while being considerate of their individual temperament. For instance, expecting a shy child to overcome their shyness instantly by sending them to a week-long summer camp is unrealistic. Instead, gradual and supportive interactions are more effective in helping them develop confidence and social skills.

1. Gradual Social Exposure: Begin with small, manageable social interactions. For example, invite one or two friends over for a playdate rather than enrolling them in a large group activity. This allows the child to practice social skills in a less overwhelming setting.

2. Family Activities: Engage in family-based activities that involve teamwork and communication, such as preparing a meal together or working on a family project. This provides a safe environment for the child to practice social interactions and cooperation, which aligns with the Islamic value of family unity and cooperation.

3. Role-Playing Games: Use role-playing games to simulate various social situations. For instance, practice greeting visitors, asking for help, or resolving conflicts. This helps the child become more comfortable with different social scenarios and mirrors the Islamic practice of respectful communication.

4. Islamic Community Involvement: Encourage participation in local Islamic community events, such as volunteering at the mosque or joining youth groups. This not only helps build social skills but also reinforces the importance of contributing to the community, as emphasized in the teachings of the Prophet Muhammad (peace be upon him) about charity and community service.

5. Seek Professional Support: If necessary, consult with a child psychologist or counselor who understands Islamic values to help your child develop social skills in a supportive and culturally sensitive

manner. This aligns with the Islamic principle of seeking knowledge and assistance to overcome challenges.

By following these practical steps and reflecting the Islamic values of patience, empathy, and gradual development, you can guide your child towards forming healthy and respectful relationships, aligned with the teachings of Islam.

Reality-testing abilities refer to a person's capacity to understand and assess the real-world consequences of their actions and decisions. This involves recognizing the cause-and-effect relationships between their behavior and its outcomes, and making adjustments based on this awareness. Developing these abilities helps individuals make informed choices and learn from their experiences.

In children, reality-testing abilities help them understand that their actions have tangible consequences. For example, if a child leaves their toys outside in the rain, they will get damaged. By experiencing these outcomes, children learn to anticipate the results of their actions and adjust their behavior accordingly.

In an Islamic context, fostering reality-testing abilities aligns with the teachings of accountability and personal responsibility. For instance, the Quran and Hadith emphasize the importance of being mindful of one's actions and their consequences, encouraging individuals to act with wisdom and foresight. This helps children grow into responsible adults who understand the impact of their actions on themselves and others, in line with Islamic values.

Two widely recognized discipline techniques—natural consequences and logical consequences—are effective in helping children develop their reality-testing abilities. Natural consequences occur without any parental intervention and stem from cause-and-effect situations. For example, if a child neglects to wear their raincoat on a rainy day, they will get wet. If they don't complete their chores, their room will stay messy. Ignoring the rules during playtime might result in losing a game. Similarly, if they forget to store their bike properly, it might get damaged. It is essential not to shield your child from these natural consequences unless they pose a health or safety risk. For instance, allowing a child to play with matches to teach fire safety is dangerous. However, allowing them to experience being wet, having a messy room, or missing out on a game can be a valuable learning opportunity, as long as it does not jeopardize their well-being.

Logical consequences, on the other hand, require parental intervention and should be directly related to the misbehavior. For example, if your child neglects to put their dirty dishes in the sink after a meal, it is logical for them to help clean up the kitchen afterward. While overseeing this task, remain neutral and avoid punitive remarks like, "I told you so." Ensuring the consequence is logically tied to the behavior teaches the child that they must acknowledge the consequences of their actions, even if they find them inconvenient.

Examples from Common Sense and Islamic Perspective:

1. Natural Consequence of Forgetting a School Project: If a child forgets to bring their homework to school, they may face a lower grade or a reprimand from their teacher. This experience helps them understand the importance of responsibility and preparation, reflecting the Islamic value of fulfilling one's duties (as emphasized in Surah Al-Mulk, 67:15).

2. Logical Consequence of Neglecting to Feed Pets: If a child fails to feed their pet, the logical consequence would be that they have to take on the responsibility of caring for the pet more attentively for a week. This teaches them about responsibility and accountability, consistent with the Islamic teaching of caring for animals as highlighted in the Hadith of the Prophet Muhammad (peace be upon him).

3. Natural Consequence of Not Dressing Appropriately for Weather: If a child refuses to wear a jacket on a cold day, they will feel cold. This helps them understand the importance of dressing appropriately, aligning with the Islamic principle of taking care of one's health (as advised in various Hadiths).

4. Logical Consequence of Not Returning Borrowed Items: If a child borrows a toy from a friend and fails to return it, a logical consequence would be that they need to help with organizing or maintaining shared toys. This teaches them the value of trust and respect in relationships, reflecting the Islamic teaching of fulfilling promises and being honest.

5. Natural Consequence of Ignoring Personal Hygiene: If a child neglects their personal hygiene, such as not brushing their teeth, they might experience discomfort or dental issues. This teaches them the importance of personal care, which is supported by the Islamic teaching of cleanliness being half of faith (as stated in the Hadith of the Prophet Muhammad, peace be upon him).

6. Natural Consequence of Overindulging in Sweets: If a child eats too many sweets, they might experience a stomach ache. This helps them learn about moderation and the effects of their dietary choices, aligning with the Islamic principle of moderation and balance in eating (as emphasized in the Hadith of the Prophet Muhammad, peace be upon him).

7. Logical Consequence of Not Doing Homework: If a child consistently fails to complete their homework, a logical consequence could be that they must stay after school to complete it. This teaches them about the importance of fulfilling their educational responsibilities and the impact of their actions on their academic performance.

8. Natural Consequence of Mismanaging Time: If a child spends too much time playing video games and neglects their study time, they may find themselves unprepared for a test. This helps them understand the importance of time management and prioritization, reflecting the Islamic value of managing one's time wisely (as advised in various Hadiths).

9. Logical Consequence of Ignoring Household Rules: If a child ignores household rules such as not running inside the house, a logical consequence might be having to miss out on a favorite activity. This teaches them about the importance of following rules and the consequences of ignoring them, reflecting the Islamic teaching of adhering to rules and regulations.

10. Natural Consequence of Not Listening to Instructions: If a child does not follow safety instructions while using playground equipment, they might get hurt. This experience helps them understand the importance of listening to instructions and safety guidelines, aligning with the Islamic principle of protecting oneself and others from harm (as emphasized in the teachings of Islam).

By incorporating these discipline techniques and practical examples within an Islamic framework, you can guide your child in developing responsible behavior and a deeper understanding of their actions and consequences, consistent with Islamic teachings.

IT IS IMPORTANT THAT parents teach thir children to develop problem-solving abilities, incorporating Islamic principles and practical strategies:

1. Encourage Critical Thinking through Stories: Share stories from the Quran and Hadith that illustrate problem-solving and wisdom. For instance, narrate the story of Prophet Yusuf (Joseph) and his

interpretation of dreams in prison, highlighting how he relied on Allah and used his knowledge to address complex situations.

2. Model Problem-Solving Skills: Demonstrate problem-solving in daily life. For example, when deciding on how to organize a family event or solve a household issue, involve your child in the planning process, explaining how you seek Allah's guidance and make decisions.

3. Teach through Islamic History: Discuss the strategies and decisions of the Prophet Muhammad (peace be upon him) and his companions in addressing various challenges. For instance, how the Prophet addressed the issues during the Battle of Badr shows practical problem-solving and leadership skills.

4. Use Role-Playing: Create scenarios for your child to practice problem-solving. For example, role-play a situation where they need to address a disagreement with a friend, guiding them to find a resolution aligned with Islamic teachings.

5. Encourage Independent Decision-Making: Allow your child to make age-appropriate decisions, such as choosing a hobby or setting up a small family event. Support them in assessing their options and making choices while reflecting on Islamic principles.

6. Teach Dua and Reliance on Allah: Encourage your child to make Dua (supplication) when facing difficulties and to trust in Allah's plan. Explain that while they seek solutions, they should also turn to Allah for help and guidance.

7. Provide Opportunities for Real-Life Problem-Solving: Engage your child in activities that require problem-solving, such as organizing a community service project or planning a family gathering. This allows them to apply their problem-solving skills in practical settings.

8. Discuss and Reflect: After resolving an issue, discuss with your child what strategies worked and what could be improved. Reflect on how Islamic teachings influenced their approach and decision-making process.

9. Encourage Teamwork: Foster teamwork through group activities where your child collaborates with others to solve problems. This could include group study sessions or community projects, highlighting the importance of cooperation and mutual support in Islam.

10. Praise and Positive Reinforcement: Acknowledge and praise your child's problem-solving efforts. Positive reinforcement motivates them to continue developing their skills and applying Islamic values in their approach to challenges.

Impulse control in Muslim children involves the ability to manage and regulate their immediate reactions, emotions, and desires in line with Islamic principles. This skill is crucial for their development, helping them make thoughtful decisions and act in accordance with Islamic values. Here's an exploration of impulse control from an Islamic viewpoint:

1. Understanding Impulse Control

Impulse control includes:

- Waiting for Greater Rewards: The ability to delay immediate gratification in favor of more significant benefits later.

- Managing Emotions: Controlling and expressing feelings appropriately.

- Making Considered Decisions: Reflecting on the potential outcomes of actions before proceeding.

2. Islamic Teachings on Self-Control

Islam underscores self-control and patience as admirable traits:

- Quranic Principles: The Quran speaks about the virtues of patience and restraint. For example, in Surah Al-Baqarah (2:286), believers are encouraged to exercise patience during trials. Surah Al-Asr (103:2-3) emphasizes patience and righteous deeds as keys to success.

- Prophetic Role Models: The Prophet Muhammad (peace be upon him) exemplified exceptional self-control. His patience and forgiveness, even in difficult situations, serve as valuable lessons in managing impulses.

3. Methods for Enhancing Impulse Control

1. Demonstrate Self-Control: Children observe and learn from their parents. Show how to handle emotions and make measured decisions. For instance, when encountering a stressful situation, manage your responses calmly and discuss your approach with your child.

2. Use Islamic Narratives: Share stories from the Quran and Hadith that reflect self-control. For example, recount how Prophet Yusuf (Joseph) maintained patience and self-discipline despite facing severe trials and temptation.

3. Encourage Focus in Worship: Foster mindfulness and concentration during Salah (prayer) and other religious practices. This focus helps build patience and impulse control, which are beneficial in other areas of life.

4. Implement Consistent Routines: Create and maintain structured daily routines to provide clear guidelines for behavior. This helps children understand expectations and develop self-discipline.

5. Affirm Positive Behavior: Praise and reward your child when they show self-control. Acknowledge their efforts to manage their impulses and follow rules, reinforcing positive behavior.

6. Guide with Dua: Teach your child to make Dua (supplication) for assistance in controlling their impulses. Specific prayers can be introduced to seek Allah's help in maintaining patience and self-discipline.

7. Provide Practice Scenarios: Offer opportunities for your child to practice impulse control in real situations, such as waiting for their turn in activities or managing conflicts calmly. Guide them through these situations to help them learn effective strategies.

8. Explain Consequences: Use examples from the Quran and Hadith to show the effects of impulsive actions. Help your child understand the repercussions of their behavior on themselves and others.

9. Reflect on Experiences: After a situation where impulse control was tested, discuss with your child what happened. Review what was done well, what could be improved, and how to handle similar situations more effectively in the future.

10. Develop Emotional Awareness: Help your child recognize and understand their emotions. By identifying their feelings and triggers, they can better manage their impulses and make thoughtful choices.

Applying these strategies within an Islamic framework supports the development of impulse control in Muslim children, enhancing their overall well-being and ensuring their actions align with Islamic teachings.

Parenting out of fear can manifest in various ways, often leading to anxiety, overprotectiveness, or inconsistent discipline. Here are some examples of how fear-driven parenting might appear:

1. Overprotection

Scenario: A parent prevents their child from participating in activities like sports or social gatherings out of fear that the child might get hurt or face negative experiences.

Example: A mother might not allow her child to play soccer with friends because she is anxious about potential injuries or accidents, limiting the child's opportunities for physical activity and social interaction.

2. Excessive Control

Scenario: A parent exerts excessive control over their child's choices and actions, fearing that the child might make poor decisions or face failure.

Example: A father dictates every aspect of his teenager's life, including their choice of friends, extracurricular activities, and even career path, out of fear that the child might make mistakes or face failure.

3. Fear-Based Discipline

Scenario: Discipline strategies are based on fear rather than constructive guidance, leading to a punitive approach rather than one that promotes understanding and growth.

Example: A parent uses threats and harsh punishment, such as yelling or grounding, to control behavior because they fear that any misstep will lead to serious negative outcomes.

4. Avoiding Challenges

Scenario: A parent avoids exposing their child to challenges or difficulties due to fear of failure or disappointment.

Example: A parent does the child's homework for them or intervenes in school projects to ensure they get perfect grades, fearing that their child's failure will reflect poorly on them or harm the child's future.

5. Overemphasis on Safety

Scenario: A parent's fear of potential dangers leads them to overly emphasize safety, which can limit the child's exploration and development.

Example: A parent might excessively worry about their child's safety during everyday activities, such as playing outside or riding a bike, and impose overly restrictive rules to prevent any perceived risk.

6. Inconsistent Expectations

Scenario: Fear leads to inconsistent enforcement of rules and expectations, which can confuse the child and lead to behavioral issues.

Example: A parent might sometimes ignore a child's misbehavior out of fear of conflict, but at other times react harshly, creating an unpredictable environment that can be unsettling for the child.

7. Over-Validation

Scenario: A parent excessively validates their child's every achievement and protects them from criticism out of fear of damaging their self-esteem.

Example: A parent constantly praises their child's every action and shields them from any form of constructive criticism, fearing that negative feedback might harm the child's confidence or motivation.

8. Micromanaging

Scenario: A parent micromanages every aspect of their child's life due to fear of them making mistakes or encountering failure.

Example: A parent insists on approving every detail of their child's social interactions or schoolwork, fearing that without their constant oversight, the child might experience setbacks or fail to meet expectations.

9. Avoiding Discussions about Difficult Topics

Scenario: Fear of negative emotions or uncomfortable conversations leads parents to avoid discussing important or challenging topics with their children.

Example: A parent avoids talking about sensitive issues such as relationships or future plans, fearing that addressing these topics might create stress or conflict.

10. Overemphasis on Perfection

Scenario: A parent's fear of their child not meeting high standards leads to an overemphasis on perfection, often creating unrealistic expectations.

Example: A parent pressures their child to excel in every academic subject and extracurricular activity, fearing that anything less than perfection will lead to failure or disappointment.

Addressing Fear-Based Parenting

To address these issues, parents can:

- Seek Knowledge and Guidance: Learn about effective parenting strategies and seek advice from experienced individuals or professionals.

- Trust in Allah's Wisdom: Rely on faith and trust in Allah's plan, recognizing that some challenges are a natural part of growth.

- Focus on Balance: Implement balanced parenting approaches that combine guidance with flexibility, allowing children to learn from their experiences while providing support and structure.

Engaging in arguments with your child can undermine your authority in multiple ways. If you lose your temper, it may teach your child that they can control your emotions through defiance, potentially leading them to provoke you intentionally. Additionally, each minute spent in argument is a minute your child avoids fulfilling your request. They might use the argument to delay the task and distract you from the original instruction.

Consider this scenario:

Mother: It's time to stop playing with your toys and start your homework.

Child: I'll do it in a little while.

Mother: No, I need you to start your homework now!

Child: You always tell me what to do! You never let me have any fun.

Mother: If you would just start your homework, I wouldn't need to keep reminding you.

Child: I don't even understand why it's so urgent. I can finish it later.

Mother: The work is piling up, and it's getting messy.

In this situation, every minute the mother spends debating whether it's urgent to start homework or whether she's being too controlling delays the child from doing the homework. Such arguments give the child more control and prolong the task.

Here's a more effective approach:

Mother: It's time to stop playing and start your homework.

Child: I'll do it in a little while.

Mother: If you don't start your homework now, you won't be able to read your favorite book later today.

Child: You're always like a drill sergeant! You never let me enjoy myself.

At this point, the mother should wait briefly to see if the child will comply. If the child does not begin their homework, the mother should follow through with taking away the favorite book. By setting a clear boundary with one warning and being ready to enforce the consequence, the mother shows that she is in control.

Although giving just one warning might seem strict, enforcing the consequence reinforces that arguing or delaying instructions is ineffective. It shows the child that they cannot manipulate your reactions, only their own behavior. By avoiding power struggles, you teach your child that they can control their actions but cannot dictate your responses.

Repeatedly shouting, "Do it now!" to force a child to start their homework will only escalate the situation, giving the child more power as you lose your composure and resort to more drastic measures. Instead, maintain calm authority and use clear, consistent consequences to guide your child's behavior effectively.

Allowing Muslim children to make mistakes and learn from them is essential for their growth and development, in line with Islamic principles that emphasize learning from experience. Here's how you can support your child in making mistakes and learning from them, reflecting Islamic teachings:

1. Encourage Learning from Mistakes

Islamic Perspective: The Prophet Muhammad (peace be upon him) taught that making mistakes is part of the human experience and that learning from them is a path to improvement. He said, "Every son of Adam is a sinner, and the best of sinners are those who repent" (Sunan Ibn Majah).

Practical Approach: Allow your child to face new challenges and make mistakes in a safe environment. Engage in open and constructive discussions about the mistake, focusing on lessons learned rather than the error itself.

2. Promote Reflection and Repentance

Islamic Perspective: Self-reflection and seeking forgiveness are crucial in Islam. Allah says in the Quran, "Indeed, Allah loves those who are constantly repentant and loves those who purify themselves" (Quran 2:222).

Practical Approach: After a mistake, help your child reflect on what happened and how they can improve. Encourage them to make Dua (supplication) for guidance and forgiveness, showing them that seeking Allah's help is part of their growth process.

3. Teach Responsibility

Islamic Perspective: Islam places emphasis on personal responsibility and accountability. The Prophet Muhammad (peace be upon him) said, "Each of you is a shepherd and each of you is responsible for his flock" (Sahih Bukhari).

Practical Approach: Allow your child to take responsibility for their actions and decisions. Help them understand the consequences of their mistakes and guide them in finding solutions, fostering a sense of ownership and accountability.

4. Support with Compassion

Islamic Perspective: Compassion and understanding are key in Islam. Allah says in the Quran, "And lower to them the wing of humility out of mercy" (Quran 17:24).

Practical Approach: Approach your child's mistakes with empathy and support. Reassure them that making mistakes is a natural part of learning, and provide help without judgment, showing that you are there to support them through their learning process.

5. Foster a Growth Mindset

Islamic Perspective: Islam encourages continuous improvement and striving for excellence. Allah says, "So be patient. Indeed, the promise of Allah is truth" (Quran 30:60).

Practical Approach: Encourage your child to view mistakes as opportunities for growth rather than failures. Emphasize that learning and striving to improve are valuable aspects of their journey, and that success often comes from perseverance and effort.

6. Celebrate Efforts and Progress

Islamic Perspective: Islam values effort and striving in the right direction. The Prophet Muhammad (peace be upon him) said, "The strong person is not the one who is good at wrestling; rather, the strong person is the one who controls himself when he is angry" (Sahih Bukhari).

Practical Approach: Recognize and celebrate your child's efforts and progress, regardless of the outcome. This positive reinforcement helps build their confidence and encourages them to continue trying and learning.

7. Set a Positive Example

Islamic Perspective: The Prophet Muhammad (peace be upon him) exemplified humility and resilience in facing challenges with patience and faith.

Practical Approach: Demonstrate how to handle mistakes with grace and constructive attitude. Show your child that everyone makes errors and that what matters is how one responds to and learns from them.

By integrating these principles into your parenting, you align with Islamic values, fostering your child's personal growth and resilience while maintaining a supportive and compassionate approach.

Father: Ahmed, can we talk about something important?

Ahmed: Sure, Dad. What's up?

Father: I want to discuss why managing stress is so crucial. You know, in Islam, patience and perseverance are highly valued. Allah says in the Quran, "O you who have believed, seek help through patience and prayer. Indeed, Allah is with the patient" (Quran 2:153). This means enduring difficulties with patience and trusting Allah is key to overcoming challenges.

Ahmed: I see. But sometimes, I feel so overwhelmed, especially with school and exams.

Father: I understand. When you manage stress well, you're better able to face challenges and succeed. For example, if you're preparing for an important exam and you get too stressed out, it can make it hard to focus. You might feel tired and even get sick, which can make you miss school and fall behind. This creates a cycle where stress leads to more stress. So, you should prepare everyday for the exams right from the beginning of the school. Then later during the exams you would not need to do any extra study. You just would need to revise. So, by doing the thing that you dislike that is studying everyday consistently from the beginning when other children would be playing and not worrying about their exams, you will avoid increased stress later on. So, take less stress now by hard word everyday and avoid the massive build up of stress later on. You can suffer little by little everyday and study even if you don't like to study now when there are no exams, and avoid the huge suffering later during exams.

Ahmed: That makes sense. So, how can I handle stress better?

Father: Well, it's about learning to manage your stress without letting it overwhelm you. By reducing your stress reactivity, you lower the levels of cortisol, the stress hormone, in your body. If you don't manage it well, high cortisol levels can make you feel more tired and increase your chances of getting sick.

Ahmed: How can I start managing stress better?

Father: Start by practicing patience and turning to prayer when you're feeling overwhelmed. Remember, seeking help through patience and prayer is encouraged in our faith. Also, try to stay focused and take things one step at a time. It's important to balance your efforts and take care of your health. By doing this, you'll be better prepared to face challenges and maintain your well-being. Have you heard of something called distress tolerance?"

Ahmed: "No, what's that?"

Father: "Distress tolerance is the ability to endure and manage emotional pain and stress in a healthy way. It means handling tough situations without letting them overwhelm you or turning to harmful behaviors."

Ahmed: "How can I get better at that?"

Father: "There are several key aspects to distress tolerance. First, there's acceptance. It's important to acknowledge and accept your emotions, even if they're uncomfortable. Realizing that feeling stressed is a normal part of life helps you face it more calmly."

Ahmed: "So, I shouldn't try to ignore how I feel?"

Father: "Exactly. Trying to avoid your feelings can make them stronger. Instead, you can practice mindfulness—being aware of your emotions and focusing on the present moment without judging yourself. This helps reduce the intensity of the distress."

Ahmed: "That makes sense. What about when I'm feeling really overwhelmed?"

Father: "In those moments, you can use self-soothing techniques like deep breathing or engaging in activities that make you happy. These methods help calm your immediate emotional responses."

Ahmed: "And if there's a problem causing the stress?"

Father: "Good question. You can use problem-solving strategies to address and resolve the issue. Finding practical steps to manage or change the situation can help reduce your stress."

Ahmed: "What if I'm having trouble controlling my emotions?"

Father: "That's where emotional regulation comes in. It involves understanding and adjusting your reactions. Recognizing what triggers your emotions and finding healthy ways to express them is key."

Ahmed: "And what if I just need someone to talk to?"

Father: "Reaching out for help is important. Support seeking means talking to family, friends, or teachers who can provide guidance and emotional support. It's always okay to ask for help when you need it."

Ahmed: "Thanks, Baba. I feel better knowing there are ways to handle stress more effectively."

Father: "You're welcome, Ahmed. Remember, developing these skills can help you manage life's challenges more effectively. We can always work on these together."

Ahmed: "I'd like that. JazakAllah Khair for the advice."

Father: "JazakAllah Khair to you too, my son. May Allah guide and support you through all challenges."